Challenging Logic Puzzles

**Official Mensa
Puzzle Book**

Puzzles

Barry R. Clarke

Illustrated by Rob Collinet

Sterling Publishing Co., Inc.
New York

Acknowledgments

I would like to thank Val Gilbert, Puzzle Editor for *The Daily Telegraph* (UK), without whom the motivation to create some of these puzzles might never have arisen. I am grateful to Peter Gordon, Puzzles Editor at Sterling, for providing the opportunity to create this work. I would also like to extend my gratitude to Denis Borris and Frank Mullin, who have tested some of these puzzles on the Puzzles Forum of my website.

Mensa and the distinctive table logo are trademarks of American Mensa, Ltd. (in the U.S.), British Mensa, Ltd. (in the U.K.), and Mensa International Limited, Ltd. (in other countries) and are used by permission.

Mensa as an organization does not express an opinion as being that of Mensa or have any ideological, philosophical, political or religious affiliations. Mensa specifically disclaims any responsibility for any liability, loss or risk, personal or otherwise, which is incurred as a consequence, directly or indirectly, of the use and application of any of the contents of this book.

Edited by Claire Bazinet

Library of Congress Cataloging-in-Publication Data
Clarke, Barry R.
  Challenging logic puzzles / Barry R. Clarke.
    p. cm.
  Includes index.
  ISBN 1-4027-0541-7
  1. Logic puzzles. I. Title.
GV1493.C532 2003
793.73 dc21
                        2003006555

10 9 8 7 6

Published by Sterling Publishing Co., Inc.
387 Park Avenue South, New York, NY 10016
© 2003 by Barry R. Clarke
Distributed in Canada by Sterling Publishing,
c/o Canadian Manda Group, 165 Dufferin Street,
Toronto, Ontario, Canada M6K 3H6
Distributed in the United Kingdom by GMC Distribution Services,
Castle Place, 166 High Street, Lewes, East Sussex, England BN7 1XU
Distributed in Australia by Capricorn Link (Australia) Pty. Ltd.
P.O. Box 704, Windsor, NSW 2756, Australia

Manufactured in the United States of America
All rights reserved

Sterling ISBN-13: 978-1-4027-0541-0
       ISBN-10: 1-4027-0541-7

For information about custom editions, special sales, premium and corporate purchases, please contact Sterling Special Sales Department at 800-805-5489 or specialsales@sterlingpub.com.

CONTENTS

Introduction 4

Puzzles 6

ABOUT THE AUTHOR

BARRY R. CLARKE has written a regular column for *The Daily Telegraph* (UK) as well as several books of original puzzles. Indeed, his website http://barryispuzzled.com is one of the most popular puzzle sites on the Web. In addition to being an innovative puzzle designer, he has written comedy sketches for BBC TV, won awards as a short film maker, and is an accomplished mathematics tutor, guitarist, cartoonist and website designer. His other skills include juggling three balls, and making a playing card or coin disappear before your eyes!

Barry holds a Masters degree in Quantum Mechanics with published papers on perturbation methods and is currently working on a revision of the theory of the hydrogen atom. Despite this, he still has time to feed his cat Tigger.

Introduction

I can guarantee that this book of logic puzzles will make you think and I'll stake my socks that your neurons will be better connected by the end of it. I also hope that it makes you smile.

The puzzles in this book have either been taken from my Brain Jammer column in *The Daily Telegraph* (UK) or have been specially created. Various logic puzzle types appear within these covers, including several advanced liar puzzles that are sure to test the reader. Many examples of my Mix-and-Match logic puzzles have also been included, where rows and columns of items are presented, together with relationships between them. The aim in these puzzles is to find their correct order. Although each item is given in the correct column, only a certain number of items in each column is correctly positioned. The first example of this type of puzzle was published in *The Daily Telegraph* (UK) on May, 21, 1994, and it has proved very popular. The level of puzzle difficulty increases as the pages turn, so even expert solvers can look forward to some mind-stretching moments as they progress.

When you think you've succeeded, or puzzled about as much as you care to, turn to the solution given at the back of this book. An index is provided, allowing you to go from puzzle to solution and back again, ad infinitum if you wish, to check your own logical thought patterns against ours.

BARRY R. CLARKE
Oxford, UK
http://barryispuzzled.com

Beating at Eating

	Name	Surname	Dessert
1	Agatha	Greed	cream puffs
2	Bugsy	Forager	trifle
3	Delilah	Eatalot	cheesecake
4	Chuck	Hunk	ice cream

Four friends held a competition to see who could eat the greatest amount of dessert in weight. So they went to the Pigout Diner, ordered their preferred dessert in abundance, and the battle commenced. The results are recorded above; however, the friends ended up insensible after having crammed themselves with the richness. So, although each item is in the correct column above, the friends only managed to write down one item in each column in the correct position. The following facts are true about the correct order.

1) Chuck is one place above ice cream.
2) Trifle is not above Delilah.
3) Greed is two places below Delilah.
4) Trifle is one place above Forager.

Can you give the correct first name, surname, and dessert for each position?

Solution on page 60.

The Colored Ties

There are six colored ties: one red, two yellow, and three green. Three friends have each had earplugs put in and a blindfold put on them. Then one of the ties, selected at random, has been put on each and they have all been set facing each other with the blindfolds removed so that each can only see the other two ties. Alan says, "My tie is one of two colors." Bert says, "My tie is one of three colors." Callum says, "My tie is one of three colors."
What are the colors of their ties?

Solution on page 93.

The Four Robbers

A   **B**   **C**   **D**

Willie Wimper had just seen four men rob the Buckstown bank and had made a drawing of each man, marked A to D, for the police. The faces consisted of four rows of hair, eyes, noses, and mouths. However, Willie had only managed to get one item correctly positioned in each row. The following facts are true about the correct order.

1) Hair C is one place to the right of eyes C.
2) Eyes D are two places to the left of nose C, which is one to the right of mouth A.
3) Hair B is one place to the right of nose B, which is two places to the left of mouth D.

Can you correctly position the hair, eyes, nose, and mouth of each robber?

Solution on page 94.

Fair's Fair

Gisyerbucks Fair had arrived in town. "Step right up, step right up, ladies and gentlemen!" shouted one stall owner. "A prize for guessing the number of balls under the cups!"

On the counter in front of him were four overturned cups. Each concealed the same number of balls. On each cup was a statement about the number of balls underneath. From left to right they read as follows:

"One or four," "two or four," "two or three," and "one or two." Only one of the four statements was correct.

How many balls were under each cup, and which statement was true?

Solution on page 71.

The Greatest Human Being

	First Name	Surname	Specialty
1	Isaac	Newtune	welder
2	Albert	Eyeline	gardener
3	Marie	Curious	cleaner
4	Charles	Darling	bricklayer

In a survey to find the greatest human being, the top four people together with their specialty subject were listed in *Clock* magazine. However, a printer's error resulted in only one entry in each column being correctly positioned. The following facts could be relied upon.

1) Albert was two places above the bricklayer.
2) Darling was one place below Charles.
3) Curious was two places below the welder.

Can you find the first name, surname, and specialty for each position?

Solution on page 79.

Court Napping

	Title	Name	Favorite Game
1	Princess	Yawny	hearts
2	Duke	Driftoff	rummy
3	King	Bleereye	gin
4	Queen	Mutter	bridge
5	Earl	Outovit	poker

At Aceyduce Palace, the royal residents were in the habit of periodically sitting down to long bouts of cardplaying, often lasting into the wee hours of the morning. Naturally, they were almost always the worse for wear the next day. One morning, a courtier, interested in discovering who was affected the most by such long card-playing marathons, recorded the order in which each of the royals climbed out of bed. Unfortunately, he had also kept an eye on them throughout the play, and was so sleepy himself that although he listed each item in the correct column, he only managed to position one item correctly in each column. The following facts are true about the correct order.

1) Earl is one place after Mutter.
2) Outovit is one place before bridge.
3) King is neither Mutter nor bridge.
4) Hearts is one place before Bleereye who was two places after King.
5) Princess is two places before poker.

Can you find the correct title, name, and drink for each position?

Solution on pages 92–93.

Alien Mutations 1

Shown above are nine mutation chambers labelled A to I, surrounded by alien figures. Actually, each of the three aliens on the left has passed through the three chambers directly to their right and has been transformed into the alien on the right (e.g., the figure to the left of A has moved through chambers A, B, and C to finish as the one to the right of C). Similarly, each of the three aliens shown above the chambers has passed through the three chambers directly below to finish as seen at the bottom. It's known that each chamber effects only a single alteration (changes head or body shape, adds or removes appendages, and such).

What does each of the nine chambers do?

Solution on page 59.

The Witch's Pudding

Winnie the Witch had a habit of lodging in people's broom closets where she would experiment with her vile concoctions. On one occasion she had five ingredients ready to put in a pudding. The volume of dishwater was one half of the cauldron volume, the castor oil was one third, the dirty snow was one quarter, the crushed pig's ear was one fifth, and the sheep droppings were one sixth. The total volume of the second and third ingredients was less than half of the cauldron volume. The castor oil was added later than the crushed pig's ear but earlier than the dishwater. The dirty snow was added two places after the sheep droppings. Of course, the cauldron spilled over!

In what order were the ingredients added?

Solution on page 93.

Colored Order

Bigmouth Bertha had been given a bag of gobstoppers by her mother to stop her whining. The bag contained nine colored sweets: three red, three yellow, and three green. Bertha removed three sweets from the bag, one at a time. Her brother, Boring Bernard, who was a collector of insignificant details, noted the following four facts in his diary.

a) The first and third sweets were not a pair of yellow and green candies.
b) A green was taken earlier than a red if and only if a yellow was removed later than a red.
c) A green was not taken later than a red.
d) The first color was different from both the second and third colors.

What were the three colors in order of removal?

Solution on pages 59–60.

Best Book Prize

	Verb 1	Noun	Verb 2	Adverb
1	Killing	Puddings	Laughing	Stupidly
2	Making	Sharks	Jumping	Loudly
3	Hitting	Cakes	Running	Cruelly
4	Shooting	Flies	Hopping	Quickly

The guests had arrived for the awarding of the annual Best Book prize. White shirts, black bow ties, and brushed suits gathered around tables as the announcer came to the microphone with the results of this prestigious competition. He quickly realized, however, that although the piece of paper before him had the correct entries in each column for the four book titles (nonsensical titles each, strangely enough, consisting of four words having similar grammatical relationships), only one item in each column was correctly positioned. The following facts are true about the correct order.

1) Jumping is not adjacent to Running.
2) Sharks is one place below Loudly.
3) Killing is one place above Quickly.
4) Sharks is not in the same book title as Running.
5) Making is one place below Jumping.
6) Cakes is one place above Running.

Can you find each of the four book titles together with their position?

Solution on page 92.

The Dragemround Dance

	Male First Name	Male Surname	Female First Name	Female Surname
1	Alan	Drover	Anne	Teak
2	Joe	Kerr	Emma	Dunn
3	Rob	Foulkes	Olive	Kinnear
4	Buck	Teef	Marie	Ulman

At the annual Dragemround ballroom dance competition, each male and female pair was judged on their fox-trot. The first four places were awarded prizes, but the judge's assistant only managed to get one name in each column correctly positioned. The following facts were true.

1) Foulkes was one place below Rob but two places below Marie.
2) Kinnear was two places above Olive.
3) Teak was one place below Kerr but one place above Buck.

Can you give the correct male and female first name and surname for each position?

Solution on page 83.

The Three Doors

As the audience at the Globule Theatre waited for the production to begin, the leading lady, Lipstick Lil, was nowhere to be seen. The word was that she was in either dressing room 1, 2 or 3, so the stage manager went to look for her. Unfortunately, outside each door was a minder from the Attitude Security Company, rather disagreeable looking fellows, who refused to let anyone into the rooms they were guarding.

"Where's Lipstick Lil?" the stage manager asked.
"Room 1 or 3," said the minder at room 1.
The stage manager went to room 2. "I'm looking for the leading lady."
"Room 2 or 3," said the minder.
The minder of room 3 gave a more helpful response. "She's in room 1 or 2," he said. "But exactly two of us minders are habitual liars."

If a habitual liar always lies, then in what room was the elusive Lipstick Lil?

Solution on page 59.

Whose Pet Is It?

Anita, Ben, Chuck, Debbie, Eliza, and Fred owned a parakeet, cat, dog, fish, parrot, and owl, although not necessarily in that order.

1) Eliza's neighbor, who was not Ben, owned the parrot.
2) Fred did not own a flying creature.
3) The parakeet owner lived next to Debbie.
4) Ben did not own a four-legged pet.
5) Both the owl and cat owners lived across the street from Eliza who lived next to the parakeet owner.
6) The owl and parakeet owners lived at the opposite end of the street to Anita and Ben.

Can you find the correct pet for each owner?

Solution on page 90.

Treasure Island

Blind Pugh was after hidden treasure, just like the rest of his shipmates, but could not see the map of Treasure Island. However, his hearing was shipshape, and he intended to locate the treasure from what he overheard and get there before the others. The island was divided into a 4x4 grid of equal squares, each square having a unique color. He had heard the following facts:

1) The blue square was one square horizontally to the left of the pink square.
2) The orange was one to the right of and one above the white.
3) The red was one square vertically above the purple.
4) The lavender was one square horizontally to the left of the indigo.
5) The brown was one vertically below the green.
6) The purple was one horizontally to the left of the gray.
7) The violet was two horizontally to the right of the yellow.
8) The indigo was one vertically above the white.
9) The turquoise was two below and one to the right of the red.
10) The crimson was one to the right of and one below the green.
11) The gold square indicates where the gold is buried.

Where was the gold?

Solution on pages 60–61

The Show Must Go On

	Play	Company	Location
1	Hamlet	Ditherers	London
2	Macbeth	Egomaniacs	New York
3	Julius Caesar	Amnesiacs	Ontario
4	Othello	Lovelies	Sydney

The *Daily Drivel* had just printed its list of best-attended Shakespeare productions currently being staged in various cities around the world. Its theater section was the most popular of all its features, so it was with great embarrassment that Dollars Dougan, the editor, discovered errors. Although each item was in the correct column, only one item in each column was in the correct position. The following facts were certain about the correct order.

1) Julius Caesar was one place below Ontario.
2) The Egomaniacs were one place below the Hamlet production.
3) Fourth place was not occupied by the Egomaniacs.
4) The Sydney production was two places above the Lovelies.

Can you find the correct play, theatre company and location for each position?

Solution on page 82.

Classroom Capers

	First name	Surname	Crime
1	Bottle	Pincher	defying teacher
2	Splodge	Drip	breaking windows
3	Fidget	Splutter	hitting pupils
4	Puddle	Crab	shouting obscenities

Four children who had been naughty were lined up outside the Principal's office. The principal's secretary took the first name, surname, and crime for each child and wrote it down. However, although each item appeared in the correct column, the mischievous children had mixed up their details so that only one item in each column was correctly positioned.

1) Puddle's surname was either Drip or Pincher and he either broke windows or hit people.
2) The second child's crime was neither defying teacher nor breaking windows.
3) Either Bottle or Puddle had either shouted obscenities or broken windows and the child in front of him was neither Splodge nor Puddle and was either Splutter or Pincher.
4) Either Splodge or Puddle was first in the queue.
5) Neither Splutter nor Pincher was third.

Can you give the correct first name, surname, and crime for each child in the line?

Solution on page 61.

The Beauty Contest

	Contestant	House name	Occupation
1	Ms. Myafare	Wyewurry	Sheep shearer
2	Ms. Slapinum	Duncheatin	Mud wrestler
3	Mrs. Wowie	Outasugar	Bullfighter

Cut-throat Close had a bad reputation for crime and violence so the residents decided to organize a beauty contest to try to raise the community spirit. Unfortunately, as one might expect, there was some mischief when the results were recorded. Although each item was in the correct column, one column had three items correctly positioned, one had just one item correct and one had no item correct. Police Officer Wazzup had to sort out the muddle and subsequently discovered the following facts.

1) Either Ms. Slapinum or Ms. Myafare were at Outasugar.
2) Mrs. Wowie was not first.
3) The bullfighter came just before Ms. Myafare.

Can you give the correct contestant, house name, and occupation for each position?

Solution on page 95.

18

Spy of the Year

	First Name	Surname	Code Name
1	Nick	Hing	Hadenov
2	Choo	Anfit	Fingsarov
3	Hans	Errs	Nodapov
4	Baz	Teale	Tikelikov

At the Spy-of-the-Year competition, the results had just been announced. The problem was, someone had tampered with the paper they were written on, altering the order, so that although each item was in the correct column, only one item in each column was correctly positioned. The judges could only remember the following facts about the correct order.

1) Hing was not second.
2) Nodapov was one place above Teale.
3) Neither Fingsarov nor Nodapov was first.
4) Hing was one place below Nick.
5) Neither Hans nor Nick were third.

Can you give the correct first name, surname, and code name for each position?

Solution on page 73.

Changing Words

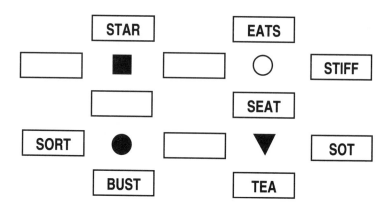

Each of the four symbols changes a word according to a definite rule as the word moves through the symbol from left to right or from top to bottom.

Can you insert the missing words in the empty boxes?

Solution on page 76.

Party Puzzle

Three friends were on their way to a party. The following facts are true about their clothes.

1) Sally did not wear leather.
2) The person in cotton was wearing yellow or blue.
3) The person in blue wore leather or wool.
4) The person in cotton was Jim or Fred.
5) Sally was not in blue.
6) Fred was in red or blue.

Can you match the person with the color and material?

Solution on page 72.

Puzzle in the Park

	Squirrel	Tree	Nuts
1	Gerald	Birch	11
2	Scamper	Sycamore	12
3	Basil	Ash	10
4	Tufty	Oak	9

Mr. Prodder, the park keeper, had spent the last few weeks observing squirrels. In fact, he had been so absorbed in watching them bury their nuts he had kept a record. The table he had made up showed the name he had assigned to the squirrel, the tree it lived in, and the number of nuts he had seen it bury, logged in order according to the bushiness of their tails. The trouble was, he had misplaced his diary and had tried to reproduce the table from memory. Although he had recalled the entries correctly, he only managed to get one entry in each column correctly positioned. The correct table had the following properties:

1) The squirrel that lived in the sycamore tree was one place below the one that had buried 12 nuts.
2) The squirrel that had buried 10 nuts was one place above Tufty.
3) The ash tree inhabitant was two places below Scamper.
4) Second place did not belong to the squirrel that had buried 10 nuts.

Can you give the name, tree, and number of nuts hidden for each position?

Solution on page 77.

Tape Teaser

	Nickname	Surname	Hometown
1	Rocky	Tryson	Boston
2	Sugar	Holyhead	Seattle
3	Basher	McCool	Texas
4	Iron	Freeman	New York

At the Annual U.S.A. Boxing Championship, the first four positions were recorded. Unfortunately, the records clerk was very drowsy from a late wedding party the night before and had mixed up the list. Although each item was in the correct column, only one item in each column was correctly positioned. The following facts are true about the correct order:

1) Freeman was one place below the boxer from Boston.
2) The fighter from Seattle was one place above the boxer nicknamed Iron.
3) McCool was two places below the contestant nicknamed Sugar.

Can you find the correct nickname, surname, and hometown for each position?

Solution on page 79.

Snow White

Snow White and the seven dwarfs, fed up with being pestered by autograph hunters, changed their names and went off to work—all eight of them, one behind the other—confident that now they would not be recognized. There were two places between Florence and Ernie, while Gertie was immediately in front of Henry. Celia was three places in front of Daniel and there were two places between Andrea and Brian. Brian was somewhere in front of Florence, Henry was somewhere in front of Celia, and Ernie was immediately in front of Andrea. Perhaps they should have changed their clothes as well because a fan ran up to the fourth from the front and shouted "You're Dopey!"

What was Dopey's pseudonym?

Solution on page 81.

Silly Pets

	Given Name	Surname	Pet
1	Twiggle	Chump	earwig
2	Mollusk	Dollup	rhinoceros
3	Polyp	Sneezer	skunk

In the local Silly Pet competition, the administrator had recorded the first three places as above. Unfortunately, although each item was in the correct column, only one item in each column was correctly positioned. The following facts were certain.

1) Either Twiggle or Mollusk, who was either Chump or Sneezer, was one place higher than either the skunk or the earwig.
2) Twiggle had neither an earwig nor a skunk.
3) Either Mollusk or Polyp was one place higher than the earwig or the rhinoceros which belonged to either Chump or Dollup.

Can you give the correct given name, surname, and pet for each position?

Solution on page 63.

Colored Cardigans

The five children of the Bright family in Gaudy Town had each bought a single-color cardigan. Unfortunately, when they got home from the shop, no one could remember which color belonged to whom. Blobby recalled that his color had six letters, Deborah knew that her color had three vowels, Eve remembered that her color ended in "e," Flash said that his was a rainbow color, and Sly claimed that his color began with a consonant. Luckily their mother had gone with them and, being bright, declared that the other colors could all be deduced only if they could discover who had the mauve cardigan. The colors were blue, mauve, orange, red, and yellow; and each color was used once only.

Can you match each child with the cardigan color?

Solution on page 67.

The Interrogation

As Shaky Sheila entered the interview room, her four interrogators—Arbuthnot, Bounder, Cad, and Drat (one of whom was a non-smoker)—sat behind the oak table polishing their questions. Sheila mentally numbered them from one to four, left to right, and noted the following facts.

1) The pipe smoker sat immediately to the right of Bounder.
2) Cad did not smoke cigarettes.
3) The cigarette smoker sat immediately to the left of Arbuthnot.
4) Cad was not the cigar smoker.
5) The cigar smoker sat immediately to the left of the cigarette smoker.
6) The cigar smoker was neither second nor third.

If no interrogator had two different smoking habits, can you find the name and smoking habit for each position?

Solution on page 69.

24

Real Ale Contest

In the International Real Ale Drinking Contest, the judge wrote down the first four contestants as follows:

	First Name	Surname	Country
1	Colin	Hogwash	Kenya
2	Denise	Earwig	Lithuania
3	Ben	Flop	Jamaica
4	Agatha	Guzzle	Ireland

The trouble was, the judge had drunk more than he should have. As a result, although each entry was in the correct column, he had only one entry in each column positioned correctly. The following facts are true about the correct order.

1) Guzzle is one place below the Lithuanian.
2) Ben is one place above the Jamaican.
3) The Jamaican is not second.
4) Colin is one place above Flop.

Can you give the correct first name, surname, and country for each position?

Solution on page 74.

Order in Class

A class of nine pupils sat at desks arranged in three rows and three columns. As viewed by the teacher at the front of the class, Oliver sat somewhere behind and in the same column as Ursula, who sat one row behind and one column to the left of George. Colin and Maggie sat at opposite ends of the same row, Colin being leftmost. George sat in the same row as Ivan while Tina sat one row behind and one column to the right of Norman.

Where was Peter sitting and what, appropriately, was the class studying?

Solution on page 70.

Breakfast on the Farm

Four animals each eat breakfast on the farm each morning. The following facts apply.

1) The horse eats in the shed or the house.
2) The animal that eats cornflakes is the horse or the cow but does not eat in the field.
3) The animal that eats in the barn has neither the toast nor the grits.
4) The goat does not eat the grits.
5) The animal that eats in the shed is the horse or the goat but does not eat toast.
6) The animal that eats the grits is not the cow and does not eat in the house.
7) The pig does not eat in the field and is not the porridge eater.
8) The cow does not eat in the house.

Can you match each animal with a breakfast and location?

Solution on page 72.

Identity Parade

Down at Copham and Shopham police station, Shifty Sid, Doubtful Des and Creepy Chris were taking part in an identity parade. Three witnesses came in one at a time and selected who they thought they had seen mugging the priest. The first said "Shifty Sid did it." The second said "Either Shifty Sid or Creepy Chris was the mugger." The third said "Neither Shifty Sid nor Doubtful Des did it." PC Neesbend knew that at least one of the witnesses had been bribed by the culprit and was lying. Fortunately, the officer knew how many were lying and managed to uniquely determine who the villain was.

Who mugged the priest?

Solution on pages 62–63.

Fancy Dress Party

	Name	Nickname	Costume	Beverage
1	Harry	Tubby	alien	coffee
2	Charles	Piggy	kangaroo	lemonade
3	William	Fly	clown	tea
4	Elizabeth	Nibble	tree	water

At the annual posh people's fancy dress party in affluent England, the host made a list of the winners. Recorded were the guest's name, nickname, fancy dress costume, and preferred beverage. Each item was in the correct column, but only one item in each column was correctly positioned. The following facts are certain about the correct order.

1) Clown is one place above water.
2) Fly is one place below William.
3) Kangaroo is not next to clown.
4) Tubby is two places above coffee.
5) Fly is not next to Tubby.
6) Elizabeth is oJ86ne place below kangaroo.

Can you find the correct name, nickname, costume, and drink for each position?

Solution on pages 86–87.

Nightmare Neighbors

	Guy	Gal	Street
1	Ed Ache	Tina Trumpet	Stubble Street
2	Arthur Brain	Anne Tagonise	Potty Place
3	Dodgy Dave	Jill Ted	Weelbee Avenue
4	Colin Names	Big Bertha	Retch Road

The local newspaper had just published the results of its Nightmare Neighbor competition. Each item appeared in the correct column, however, due to a printer's error, only one entry in each column was correctly positioned.

1) Either Jill Ted or Anne Tagonise lived at either Stubble Street or Potty Place.
2) Second place went to Ed Ache, who lived at neither Potty Place nor Retch Road, and not with Jill Ted.
3) Just after Ed Ache was neither Arthur Brain nor Colin Names, but whoever it was he lived at Stubble Street with either Tina Trumpet or Big Bertha.

Can you give the correct guy, gal, and street for each position?

Solution on page 68.

The Feed-'em-Fat Diner

	First Name	Surname	Occupation
1	Dave	Jaffa	manager
2	Connie	Fish	receptionist
3	Bill	Gateau	chef
4	Eleanor	Ingest	waiter
5	Anne	Haddock	dishwasher

At the Feed-'em-Fat Diner, the result of the most-popular-employee contest, voted for by the customers, had been decided. However, the paper which gave the results had been lost and, rather than disappoint his staff by abandoning the prize-giving, the Area Manager decided to try to recall the list. Although he managed to get each item in the correct column, he managed to get only one item in each column correctly positioned. The following facts are true about the correct order.

1) Haddock is two places below the manager.
2) Dave is two places above Ingest.
3) The waiter is two places above Anne.
4) Eleanor is three places below the receptionist.
5) Fish is not in first place.

Can you find the first name, surname, and occupation for each position?

Solution on page 80.

Trotter Farm

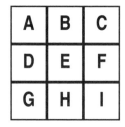

A	B	C
D	E	F
G	H	I

On Trotter Farm, the 45 pigs were kept in a 3x3 square of nine pens so that no two pens had the same number of pigs, the number in each pen was from 1–9 and each row and column totalled 15 (though not necessarily the diagonals). One day, the farmer asked his three farm hands about the number of pigs in each pen. The trouble was, they often told lies so it was no easy task to deduce the numbers.

Snout said "A has 2" and "C has 9."
Curly claimed "E has 5" and "F has 8."
Bacon announced "G has 3" and "H has 7."

One person gave two true statements, one gave only one true statement, and one gave two false statements. The farmer tried to deduce the correct numbers but, realizing he did not know which statements were false, he made no progress.
Can you find the number of pigs in each pen?

Solution on page 85.

Whodunnit?

	First name	Surname	Weapon	Location
1	James	Bracket	hammer	kitchen
2	Lyn	Thrust	rope	conservatory
3	Sid	Nutter	gun	hall
4	Alice	Kilroy	knife	library
5	Eunice	Loosenut	poison	study

Inspector Twiggit was at Muckrake mansions for the sixth time this year investigating the latest murder. The five previous murders were listed in chronological order in his notebook. However, although each item was in the correct column, only one item in each column was correctly positioned. He knew that the following facts were true.

1) Conservatory was one place below Nutter but one place above knife.
2) Gun was somewhere below Alice.
3) James was two places above Kilroy.
4) Poison was somewhere above Bracket.
5) Hall was one place below gun but one place above Eunice.
6) Alice was murdered in the library.

Can you find the correct first name, surname, murder weapon, and murder location for each position?

Solution on page 86.

Circle of Cons

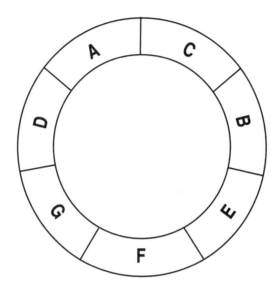

Seven convicts from the local prison had been taken out to a restaurant as a treat for not smashing up their cells for a week. To stop them from escaping, the convicts had been chained together: Andy to Bill, Bill to Colin, Colin to Dave, Dave to Ernie, Ernie to Fred, and Fred to George. However, the six chains had different lengths, chosen so that when the convicts sat down around the table for seven, and the chains were fully stretched, Andy would be six chairs from Bill, Bill five chairs from Colin, Colin four from Dave, Dave three from Ernie, Ernie two from Fred, and Fred one chair from George (that is, next to him). A prison officer incorrectly thought the seating arrangement should be as in the diagram, but in his arrangement three of the prisoners were wrongly positioned.

What is the correct seating arrangement?

Solution on page 70.

The Mermaid's Wish

One day, as Popkin was mopping his bathroom floor, he wished that life could be easier. Suddenly, a mermaid appeared in his mop bucket.

"Life *can* be easier," said the mermaid, "whenever you wish it to be. All you have to do is stand on the magic tile when you make your wish. Then any wish you make will be granted."

Now, Popkin's bathroom floor consisted of 16 square tiles arranged in a 4x4 square and, apparently, only one of them was the magic one (unfortunately, if he didn't select the correct one on the first try, the magic would dissipate). The mermaid gave Popkin instructions for finding that specific tile. To do it, he must first choose exactly four tiles so that no row or column is used more than once and no two tiles are diagonally adjacent. Then, Popkin must stand on one of three of his four chosen tiles (only three of which lead to the magic tile) and perform the only appropriate instruction of the following five (with a different direction for each of the three tiles) to reach the magic tile.

1) Step two tiles to the left.
2) Step one tile up.
3) Step one tile down.
4) Step two tiles to the right.
5) Step one tile up then one tile to the right.

Where was the magic tile?

Solution on page 61.

Logic Letters

R	L	H	E	S	T	W	G	Y	A	O

Shown is a list of eleven letters with a vacant box beneath each. Ten of the boxes must be marked with a cross, two at a time, left then right, in the following manner. First mark two boxes that are two apart (one space between), then two boxes three apart, then four apart, five apart and finally six apart so that no box is occupied by more than one cross and one letter is left unused.

There are actually several ways of doing this, but only one way, performed in the manner indicated, spells the surname of a famous writer. For example, one way is HS(2), GO(3), TA(4), EY(5), RW(6), which gives the name HSGOTAEYRW, completely meaningless.

Can you mark the boxes to reveal the name of the writer?

Solution on page 71.

Bank on Us

	Bank	Manager	Street
1	Badmove	Mr. Tremble	Daisy
2	Rippemov	Mrs. Chance	Arlington
3	Savehup	Ms. Manidge	Porcupine
4	Hirate	Mr. Fortune	Trumpet

Big Bucks Bill was trying to decide which bank to invest his $100 with. So he made a list of what he thought were the best four banks in his neighborhood. However, in his haste, he wrote down the list incorrectly. Although each item was in the correct column, only one item in each column was correctly positioned. The following facts are true about the correct order.

1) The Badmove bank is not second.
2) Porcupine Street is one place below Ms. Manidge.
3) Mr. Tremble is one place above the Hirate bank.
4) The Rippemov bank is one place below Daisy Street.
5) The manager in second place is not Mr. Tremble.

Can you find the bank, manager, and street for each position?

Solution on page 78.

Mixed Marriage

	Male	Female	Surname
1	Bob	Fiona	Ogden
2	Eddie	Jill	Marsden
3	Dan	Ivy	Levy
4	Chris	Gina	Norris
5	Andy	Harriet	Kennett

Five couples on a world cruise had just got married. The DJ at the evening party was ready to make an announcement, offering his congratulations to the couples in the order they were married. However, although each item was in the correct column, only one item in each column was correctly positioned. The following facts are true about the correct order.

1) Kennett is two places below Andy.
2) Fiona is two places above Eddie.
3) Ivy is not adjacent to Fiona.
4) Dan is one above Jill but one below Levy.
5) Marsden is two places below Ivy.

Can you give the correct male, female, and surname for each position?

Solution on pages 88–89.

Prime Time

	Performer	Action	Adverb
1	dog	tapping	softly
2	wife	laughing	loudly
3	cat	belching	aggressively
4	neighbor	whistling	timidly
5	pig	sneezing	unashamedly

The producers of the Jock Letterbox Show were meeting to discuss how they were going to boost ratings. Someone had the idea of getting a performer to do something unusual and had even made a list of possible acts. However, although each item was in the correct column, only one item in each column had been written in the correct position. The following facts are true about the correct order.

1) Laughing is two places above loudly.
2) Neither sneezing nor unashamedly are fourth.
3) The neighbor is two places below tapping.
4) Softly is not three places from loudly.
5) The cat is two places above sneezing.
6) The pig is three places below softly.

Can you find the correct performer, action, and adverb for each position?

Solution on pages 82–83.

Wildwood Grubs

In Wildwood Grubs prison, there were four cells numbered 1–4 from left to right, with only one prisoner to a cell. The following facts had been recorded in the prison officer's logbook.

1) Cell 2 was occupied by either Angry Alan or Desperate Dave.
2) The burglar was next to the poisoner but not next to the strangler.
3) Neither Brutal Bill nor Desperate Dave was the knifeman.
4) Either the strangler or the knifeman was in cell 4.
5) Brutal Bill was next to Cruel Colin.
6) Desperate Dave was to the immediate left of the strangler.

Can you find the inmate and crime for each cell?

Solution on page 69.

Being Arkward

As the animals were lining up to go into the ark, an argument broke out about which species should have priority in the queue. Teeth were bared, and soon the procession fell into disarray. Luckily, Noah arrived just in time to stop the lions eating everyone. Noah's solution was for the animals to resume their original order but no one could agree what the first five places were.

Noah correctly recalled that the giraffe was either two or three places after the rhinoceros. The pig claimed that the newt, wallaby, and orangutan appeared in the first five and that the wallaby did not appear next to the giraffe. He also said that the newt was immediately after the orangutan. The cat maintained that the horse, tiger, and iguana were in the first five, saying that neither the tiger nor the horse were next to the rhinoceros. She also said that the iguana was two places before the horse. Either the pig or the cat were lying.

What was the right order for the first five places?

Solution on page 63.

Alien Court

	Captain	Planet	Spaceship
1	Ponga	Blink	Outagas
2	Bleep	Loopy	Boldleego
3	Arial	Grunt	Rustcan
4	Tweak	Pobble	Hosspuld
5	Riddle	Ether	Supersnail

At the headquarters of Ademordna Galaxy Courthouse, five spaceship captains were up in court for not paying their parking fines. The order that the cases were to be heard had been listed giving the captain's name, his planet of origin, and the name of his spaceship. Each item was in the correct column, but only one item had been correctly positioned in each column. The following facts were certain about the correct order.

1) Boldleego was somewhere above Pobble which was not above Rustcan.
2) Ponga was one place below Grunt and one place above Outagas.
3) Arial was not at 4.
4) Blink was two places above Riddle and one above Hosspuld.

Can you give the correct captain, planet, and spaceship for each position?

Solution on page 88.

A Meal Out

	Nickname	Name	Food	Beverage
1	Doghouse	Steve	pork	milkshake
2	Bigears	Annie	lamb	latte
3	Tender	Chris	beef	cappuccino
4	Simple	Jackie	chicken	mocha
5	Wimpsy	Georgina	fish	tea

Five friends, having a meal out at a local restaurant, ordered their food and drink. The waiter, new on the job but striving for "personalized" service, wrote down the name, food, and beverage for each person in the order they occurred. He even assigned each person a nickname—he liked to be on familiar terms! Unfortunately, although each item was in the correct column, he only managed to get one entry in each column correctly positioned. The following facts are true about the correct order.

1) Annie is one place below the beef eater.
2) Pork is one place above Tender and one below tea.
3) Chris and Steve are not adjacent.
4) Fish is one place below mocha and two below Steve.
5) Neither Annie nor Doghouse are fifth.
6) Bigears is one place above latte and one below Chris.

Can you find the assigned nickname, name, food, and beverage for each position?

Solution on page 89.

Murder at Little Winkle

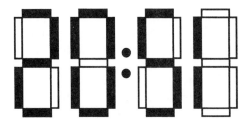

The village of Little Winkle was crawling with detectives. The body of Herbert Trudge had just been found in the woods, having been murdered the previous day. Apparently, he had been hit with a large rock, at which time his digital watch had stopped. Shown is a drawing of the digital display on the watch made by an artist at the scene. Only four locals, one of whom was named Alice, had passed through the wood that day and they were now each giving a statement about the other three locals.

The suspect who passed through the wood at 3 p.m. remarked "Either Connie or Sid is a lawyer, the other being a grocer." The one who got there at 5 p.m. said "Connie has an occupation beginning with 'G' while neither Jim nor I is a pharmacist." The local who turned up at 8 p.m. said "Either Sid or Jim lives in my street." The suspect who was there at 9 p.m. revealed "I am neither a pharmacist nor a geologist."

Detection of the murderer might seem straightforward, but watch! There is literally a twist to the mystery requiring the keen perception of a detective.

Can you find (a) the person and occupation for each time, and (b) the suspect who murdered Herbert Trudge?

Solution on page 78.

Dogs of War

At Mutt's Military Academy, the nine dogs in Pups Platoon were out on parade. As they stood to attention in a 3x3 square, sergeant-major Al Sayshun, the barracks bully, barked out the orders for them to change to the following positions.

1) Oddear in the row above Growler.
2) Evileye in the column to the right of Bumchew.
3) Aggro directly to the right of Canine.
4) Nasher in the opposite corner to Bumchew.
5) Ugly two places to the right of Yapper.
6) Canine in the column to the left of Oddear.

The sergeant-major had drilled them relentlessly all day with ruthless contempt, but as he surveyed their new positions, he suddenly realized what a dastardly dog he'd been.

What question faced him?

Solution on page 87.

P&B Club

Five elderly ladies from the Petticoat and Bloomers Club were visiting the theatre. They had booked five consecutively numbered seats in one row but had forgotten their agreed seating order. Connie and Ethel, who never sat next to each other, were arguing about the order. "I think it's Agatha, Bertha, you, me, and Denise," said Connie. However, she had only two of them correctly positioned. "Well, I think it's Agatha, Denise, you, Bertha, and me," said Ethel. This time only one was correctly placed. Failing to agree, they eventually sat in the order Agatha, Denise, Ethel, Bertha, and Connie. Only two were correctly placed.

What was their agreed seating order?

Solution on pages 84–85.

Knot's Nightmare

	Groom	Bride	Honeymoon
1	duck	gorilla	inkwell
2	cabbage	pizza	boots
3	alligator	egg	lake
4	banana	fly	keyhole

The Reverend Knot was having a nightmare about the four marriages he had performed the previous day. Instead of the real groom, bride, and honeymoon location, his imagination had performed a bizarre substitution. The next morning, he wrote down what had occurred but although he managed to get each item in the correct column, only one item in each column was correctly positioned. However, he was sure of the following facts.

1) Lake was not second.
2) Cabbage was married two places before pizza.
3) Either gorilla or pizza was fourth.
4) Either alligator or banana married just after either gorilla or pizza, who had a honeymoon in either keyhole or lake.

Can you reconstruct Knot's nightmare giving the correct groom, bride, and honeymoon location for each marriage?

Solution on pages 64–65.

Insects Inc.

	Applicant	Previous Job	Intended Position
1	millipede	detective	receptionist
2	cockroach	priest	manager
3	ant	kleptomaniac	security guard
4	beetle	gravedigger	treasurer

At Insects Inc., the secretary had written down the names of four applicants for positions in the order they were to be interviewed. The list also gave their previous and intended occupation. However, the secretary had managed to mix up the items in the list. Although each item was in the correct column, only one item in each column was correctly positioned. The following facts were certain about the correct order.

1) The security guard was not second.
2) The ant was one place above the gravedigger.
3) The beetle was one place below the security guard.
4) The ant was not first.
5) One place above the manager was the detective.

Can you give the applicant, previous job, and intended position for each entry?

Solution on page 76.

Animal Races

	Animal	Name	Prize
1	badger	Karen	Porsche
2	elephant	Harry	spoon
3	antelope	Lorna	television
4	cat	Ian	microwave
5	dog	George	carrot
6	frog	Jenny	radiator

At Booliba Village, the animals had decided to have a race between two sticks set 100 meters apart. The first six places were written down with the animal, its name, and the prize for that position. Unfortunately, although each item was in the correct column, only one item in each column was correctly positioned. The following facts are true about the correct positions.

1) Neither Badger nor George are sixth.
2) Microwave is two places below Harry and one above elephant.
3) Ian is not carrot and is not next to Lorna.
4) Spoon is three places below Ian and two below dog.
5) Porsche is one place below Lorna and one above antelope.

Can you find the correct animal, name, and prize for each position?

Solution on page 91.

The Four Badges

Four friends stand facing each other in a circle each wearing a colored badge. These have been chosen at random from two red, two yellow, and two green, a fact they are aware of. Each can only see the other three badges, and headphones ensure that no person can hear what any of the others say. Alice says "Neither Barney nor Carrie has red." Barney says "My color is one of three." Carrie says "I cannot see a green." Denzil says "My color is one of two colors."

What color badge does each person wear?

Solution on page 94.

Rollerblading

Grandpa Grumps had just informed the local police that several children were rollerblading in his driveway. However, by the time Police Officer Nickham turned up, the children had gone and Grandpa Grumps couldn't remember their faces. So Nickham rounded up five children in the neighborhood who had seen the culprits and listened to what they had to say about each other.

"Exactly two of us are liars," said Andy.
"Eddie tells lies," claimed Babs.
"Exactly two of the other kids lie," said Connie.
"The person who just spoke is a liar!" piped Danny.
"Exactly two of us tell the truth," said Eddie.

From which children can Nickham be sure to get reliable statements?

Solution on pages 67–68.

Alien Mutations 2

Shown above are twelve mutation chambers labelled A to L, surrounded by alien figures. Actually, each of the four aliens on the left have passed through the three chambers directly to their right and have been transformed into the aliens on the right (e.g., the figure to the left of A has moved through chambers A, B, and C to finish as the one to the right of C). Similarly, each of the three aliens shown above the chambers has passed through the four chambers directly below them to finish as shown at the bottom. It's known that each chamber effects only a single alteration (e.g., changes head or body shape, adds or removes appendages, and such).

What does each of the nine chambers do?

Hogweed's Pond

	Creature	Home	Rise Time	Cereal
1	otter	reeds	6 a.m.	Codflakes
2	toad	sticks	8 a.m.	Lice Krispies
3	newt	boot	10 a.m.	Flyflakes
4	perch	dam	7 a.m.	Pondpops
5	frog	hollow log	9 a.m.	Waterbix

Down at his local pond, Professor Hogweed was doing research into the breakfast habits of five pond creatures. He had listed the home, rising time, and breakfast cereal of each creature in the order he had observed them but had managed to mix up the list when writing out a copy. Although the copied list shown had each item in the correct column, only one item was correctly positioned in each column. The following facts are true about the correct order.

1) The creatures that lived in the sticks and the dam are not third and neither is the Lice Krispies eater.
2) The reeds resident is one place above the 9 a.m. riser.
3) The Pondpops diner is not last.
4) The frog is two places above the 10 a.m. riser.
5) Neither the frog nor the perch are second.
6) The newt is two places below the Lice Krispies diner.
7) The Flyflakes diner is two places above the dam resident.
8) Neither the 6 a.m. nor the 9 a.m. riser are fourth and neither is the reeds dweller.

Can you give the creature, home, rising time, and breakfast cereal for each position?

Solution on page 75.

Strange Signs

	To A	To B	To C	To D
Sign A	X	20	19	17
Sign B	19	X	18	15
Sign C	19	18	X	20
Sign D	17	19	20	X

The table above shows the distances (km) given on signposts at four villages A, B, C, D to their three neighboring villages. For example, at village B the signpost gives a distance of 19 km to village A. Each signpost has exactly three numbers on it. The trouble is, the signposts have been vandalized so that only one sign gives exactly three correct distances, one gives precisely two correct, one has exactly one correct and one has no correct distances. When the signpost is corrected, no distance between two villages is repeated between another pair of villages.

Can you state the number of correct distances on each sign?

Solution on page 71.

Man of Letters

Arthur Penn, a man of letters, had noticed something unusual about the five animals at the zoo. The species giraffe, leopard, gorilla, lynx, and monkey had names Lucy, Barbara, Gerald, Harold, and Larry, though not necessarily in that order. In comparing an animal's species and name, he noted the following:

1) Only one animal had the same initial letter in both.
2) Exactly two animals had just one letter 'r' in their name as well as exactly one letter 'r' in the name of their species.
3) Precisely two animals had the same number of letters in both.
4) Only two animals had the same final letter in both.

Can you find the name of each animal?

Solution on page 65.

Pet Places

	Pet	Street 1	Street 2
1	cat	Grunter	Road
2	dog	Hollow	Drive
3	elephant	Rubble	Crescent
4	alligator	Tempest	Avenue
5	parakeet	Apple	Walk
6	frog	Purple	Lane

Turtle Town was holding its annual Prize Pets competition and the first six places had already been decided. The pets were listed along with the street they came from, each street having a two-part name. However, the order presented to the master of ceremonies was not that decided on by the judges. The competition secretary had drunk one beer too many and although he managed to get each item in the correct column, only one item in each column was correctly positioned. The following facts were certain about the correct order.

1) Rubble was two places above the alligator and three places above Drive.
2) Neither Purple nor Tempest were fifth.
3) Avenue was one place below the dog and one place above Purple.
4) Fifth place was occupied by neither Avenue nor Lane.
5) Neither the parakeet nor the cat were second.
6) Crescent was one place below Hollow and three places above the frog.

Can you give the pet and both parts of the street name for each position?

Solution on page 81.

Fantasy Fortune

"What brings you here?" said a voice, as Toddler Toby neared the red cave. There, high in a tree, sat the Wizard of the Wood. "I've come to seek my fortune," said Toby. Suddenly, a pixie, an elf, a goblin, and a dwarf appeared in the cave entrance, each holding a black bag. "Then now is your chance," said the Wizard. "One of those bags holds 5,000 gold coins, one has 3,000, another 2,000, and the fourth has none."

> "My bag and the goblin's have the highest and lowest amounts," said the pixie.
>
> "This bag and the pixie's have a total of 5,000 coins," said the elf.
>
> "The dwarf's amount taken from my amount leaves 3,000 coins," said the goblin.
>
> "Neither I nor the pixie have the highest or lowest amounts," said the dwarf.

"And exactly two of them are lying," said the Wizard to Toby. "Choose a bag, but be careful, the bearer must be a truth teller or you cannot leave the wood."

Whose bag should Toddler Toby choose so as to get the most gold coins?

Solution on pages 68–69.

Consequences

	Male	Female	Location	Action
1	Butch	Polly	bridge	danced
2	Spike	Tania	lake	laughed
3	Monty	Coriander	field	cried
4	Quentin	Sylvia	shop	argued
5	Norman	Daisy	river	sneezed
6	Henry	Bonny	cinema	whistled

The Spotty children were playing a game of Consequences where one suggested a male name, another a female name, a third gave a location where they met, and the last said what action they performed on meeting. On completing the game, the children voted on their favorite combination. The results are shown above but they have been recorded incorrectly. Each item is in the correct column, but only one item in each column is correctly positioned. The following facts are true about the correct order.

1) Quentin is one place above Bonny.
2) Laughed is one place below Tania but one above Monty.
3) Shop was two places below Spike but three below Coriander.
4) Spike is not adjacent to Norman.
5) Field is one place below sneezed.
6) Norman is one place above whistled but two below bridge.
7) Polly is one place above argued but three above river.

Can you give the correct male, female, location, and action for each position?

Solution on pages 65–66.

The Boxing Match

Excitement grew as the crowd waited for the boxing match to commence. Fred "the Needle"—so called because of his ferocious jab—glared across the ring at his opponent Brutal Ben. Everyone thought it was an even match; however, the contest lasted only eight consecutive punches, four from each man, the last punch knocking the other man out cold.

1) Fred's left jab was three punches after Ben's left uppercut.
2) Ben threw his right jab two punches before Fred delivered a right hook.
3) At one point during the exchange it was Fred, Fred again, then Ben, then Fred.
4) Fred's right uppercut was three punches before Ben's left hook.
5) Ben's right to the body was sometime after Fred's left to the body.

In what order were the eight punches thrown and who won?

Solution on page 63.

Funny Fours

	First	Second	Third	Fourth
1	D	H	E	W
2	B	A	Z	K
3	L	R	I	Y
4	T	U	O	N
5	S	P	C	M

The Booliba tribe, renowned for their ability to laugh at just about anything, had just learned some new four-letter English words. So the elders of the tribe were called together to see which five words sounded the funniest. A missionary wrote down the order and although each letter was in the correct column, only one letter in each column was correctly positioned. The following facts are true about the correct order.

1) U is two places below B.
2) I is two places above H but one above K.
3) S and P are in the same word.
4) C is three places below L and one below N.
5) M is three places below O.

Can you find the five four-letter words together with their correct order?

Solution on page 84.

The Four Cats

Four cats had their food bowls set out from left to right in the following order: Ginger, Pickle, Sooty, and Tigger. Mrs. Haggis had five cans of cat food (chicken, lamb, rabbit, salmon, and turkey ready to give them. Each bowl was filled, no two bowls receiving the same flavor, so that one can was left unused. Now, the cats were fussy with their food and would only eat under certain conditions. If the lamb was to be eaten it had to be next to the turkey, whereas if the turkey was eaten it had to be next to the chicken. Pickle hated turkey. If the rabbit was eaten it had to be next to the salmon. Tigger hated lamb while Ginger disliked chicken. In fact, no cat would eat the chicken if turkey was anywhere to the left.

Can you discover which food each cat ate?

Solution on pages 73–74.

Cards in the Cave

The three colored cards that Globule placed on the floor represented his prediction of the first three positions in next season's soccer league. Each card had a team written on its face-down side. On each uppermost face were two statements: one about that card's final league position (first, second or third) and one statement about the face-down teams.

The blue card claimed "This card has a league position somewhere above a card with a true positional statement" and "This card is neither Pity City nor Runaround Rovers;" the green card said "This card is not adjacent in the league to a card with a false positional statement" and "One of the other cards is Definitely Disunited;" and the red card stated "This card is neither second nor third" and "Runaround Rovers is not second." One of the cards had two true statements, one had two false and the other had one of each.

What were the first three positions?

Solution on pages 66–67.

Resort to Reason

In the summer resort of Bleakpale, there were exactly four guest houses standing in a line along the seafront. Business was grim and each guest house had only one guest with each guest house run by only one landlord.

1) The landlord of Kestrelview did not live next door to his fellow landlord Bob.
2) Harry stayed at one of the end guest houses, which was not Ivorytowers.
3) Daniel, who ran the guest house just to the right of where Frances was staying, was next door to the Lavender guest house which was not at the end of the line.
4) Eunice stayed next door to Ivorytowers.
5) Bob ran the guest house next door to where Harry was staying.
6) Arthur ran a guest house that had only one guest house next door, the one where Eunice was staying.
7) Colin, Geraldine, and Jollyjapes were the remaining landlord, guest, and guesthouse.

Numbering the guest house positions 1–4 from left to right, can you find the landlord, guest, and guest house name for each position?

Solution on pages 74–75.

Mad Nomads

Every Saturday in the four-bedroomed Nomad house, the four occupants, one to each room, change bedrooms so that only one of them keeps the same room. On one particular Friday, Arnie occupied the front left bedroom, Barbara the front right one, Carrie the back left and Denzil the back right. The next day, they changed rooms just before the landlord called for the rent. When he demanded his money, each made a statement about the location of the rent.

1) "The room to my right," said Arnie.
2) "The room in front of me," claimed Barbara.
3) "The room to my left," said Carrie.
4) "The room diagonally to the right of mine," said Denzil.

The problem was, two of the tenants lied, while two told the truth. (Note: In a statement, a liar may refer to a room that does not exist, such as one "behind" or "to the left" of a back left room.)

Can you give the new occupant in each room and state who had the rent?

Solution on pages 71–72.

Alien Ages

	Name	Race	Planet	Age
1	Bleep	Tartan	Parp	213
2	Ting	Polyp	Dorb	385
3	Hoot	Bunter	Esther	706
4	Eek	Crispy	Booper	503
5	Peep	Winky	Grunt	897
6	Doodah	Fodder	Flip	32

Six galactic space people had entered the Funniest Space Face competition. The judges had recorded the alien's name, race of origin, home planet, and age for the first six places in the competition. However, a clerical error meant although each item was in the correct column, only one entry in each column was correctly positioned. The following facts are true about the correct order.

1) Grunt is one place above Fodder.
2) Booper is three places below Eek and two below 32.
3) Doodah is two places above Tartan and one below 385.
4) The 706-year-old alien is three places above Ting.
5) Peep is two places below Bunter and one above Parp.
6) Esther is one place above 213 and three above Polyp.

Can you find the correct name, race, planet, and age for each position?

Solution on pages 90–91.

SOLUTIONS

The Three Doors

Lipstick Lil is in room 3. If minder 1 lies then Lil is in room 2 and if minder 2 lies Lil is in 1. Now let us consider the two cases for minder 3. Suppose minder 3 tells the truth. Then Lil is in room 1 or 2 and the other two lie. However, this means that Lil is in both 1 and 2, which is not possible. So minder 3 lies, implying that Lil is in room 3 and there are not two liars altogether. This is consistent with minders 1 and 2 both being truthful.

Alien Mutations 1

A add arms, B head to square, C remove legs, D biped, E body to circle, F body to square, G head to circle, H remove arms, I remove antennae. Row 2, having only one visible mutation, must also contain two opposing mutations (i.e., one reversing the effect of another). There are no pairs of opposing mutations in any column. Since removing legs only appears in column 3, then this must be the same mutation that appears in row 1. The square head mutation only appears in column 2, so this is the one in row 1. The add arms mutation only appears in column 1, and this must be the one in row 1. The circular head mutation only appears in column 1, so this is the one in row 3, leaving the walk-erect biped mutation in column 1 row 2. The remove arms mutation is only in column 2, so this is the one in row 3. This leaves the remove antennae mutation in column 3 row 3. Checking column 2 shows that the body circle mutation was in row 2, and checking column 3 the body square mutation is in row 2.

Colored Order

The order is yellow, red, red. Condition (a) states that a yellow can be neither earlier nor later than a green. So both colors do not occur together in the chosen three. From condition (c), a green can be neither earlier nor later than a red. So these two colors do not occur together. We deduce that if a green occurs then all three sweets are green. However, this violates condition (d), as would all yellow or all red, so both red and yellow colors must appear in the three. From condition (b), the absence of a green implies that a yellow is not later than a red. So all yellow must be earlier than all red and condition (d) finalizes the order.

Beating at Eating

	Name	Surname	Dessert
1	Delilah	Hunk	trifle
2	Bugsy	Forager	cheesecake
3	Chuck	Greed	cream puffs
4	Agatha	Eatalot	ice cream

From (3), Delilah can be at 1 or 2. From (1), Chuck can be at 1, 2 or 3. If Chuck is at 1 or 2, no item can be correct in the first column (invalid). Therefore Chuck is at 3 and ice cream is at 4. If Delilah is at 2 (with Greed at 4), from (2) and (4), Forager must be at 3, and no item can be correct in the second column. So Delilah is at 1 (with Greed at 3). From (4), Forager can be at 2 or 4. At 4, no item is correct in the second column. So Forager is at 2, leaving Agatha at 4. In the second column, Forager is correct at 2, Hunk is wrong at 4 so is at 1, leaving Eatalot at 4. In the Dessert column, ice cream is correct at 4, cheesecake is wrong at 3 so can only be at 2, leaving cream puffs at 3.

Treasure Island

The gold was in the bottom left corner square of the map grid.

green	yellow	red	violet
brown	crimson	purple	grey
lavender	indigo	orange	turquoise
gold	white	blue	pink

From (2), (4) and (8) one row has lavender, indigo, orange, consecutively with white one square vertically below the indigo. Using (3), (6) and (9), the purple is one square vertically below the red, the gray is one horizontally to the right of the purple, and the turquoise is one vertically below the gray. From (5) and

(10), the brown is one vertically below the green and the crimson is one horizontally to the right of the brown. Together with (1) and (7), these make five jigsaw pieces that can only fit together in a 4x4 grid one way. The single vacant square is the gold.

The Mermaid's Wish

The magic tile is second from the left, second row down. Let us number the tiles from 1–16 from left to right along the rows starting with the top row. Only two sets of four starting numbers can be chosen to satisfy the conditions. These are (a) 2, 8, 9, 15 and (b) 3, 5, 12, 14. For each set we ask: What possible tiles can be reached using the five directions, for each starting tile? Let us consider set (a). For tile 2 we have 6, 4; tile 8 gives 6, 4, 12; tile 9 gives 5, 13, 11, 6; tile 15 gives 13, 11, 12. Now consider set (b). Tile 3 gives 1, 7; tile 5 gives 1, 9, 7, 2; tile 12 gives 10, 8, 16; tile 14 gives 10, 16, 11. Only for set (a) does the same finishing tile appear three times, this being 6.

Classroom Capers

	First Name	Surname	Crime
1	Splodge	Pincher	defying teacher
2	Fidget	Splutter	shouting obscenities
3	Bottle	Crab	breaking windows
4	Puddle	Drip	hitting pupils

From (3), the person above Bottle or Puddle, who is neither Splodge nor Puddle, cannot be at 1 due to (4), and cannot be at 3 due to (5). So this person must be at 2 with Bottle or Puddle who shouts obscenities or breaks windows at 3. That means that neither Splodge (at 2) or Fidget (at 3) can be correct in the first column, and Bottle cannot be at 1 due to (4), so only Puddle can be correct at 4. Therefore Bottle is at 3 and Splodge at 1, leaving Fidget at 2. Defying teacher can only be at 1 and shouting obscenities must be at 2 or 3. If it is at 3, hitting pupils is at 2 with breaking windows at 4 violating (3). So shouting obscenities is at 2, breaking windows at 3 and hitting pupils at 4. For the surname, Drip cannot be correct at 4 due to (1), so Pincher must be correct at 1. Drip, then, is at 4, Splutter at 2, and Crab at 3.

Alien Mutations 2

A remove arms, B biped, C add antennae, D remove legs, E head to square, F head to circle, G body to circle, H body to square, I add legs, J remove antennae, K quadruped, L add arms.

Columns 1 and 3 each have four unique identifiable mutations while column 2 has two unique identifiable ones and two unknown ones that must be opposite mutations. Rows 1 and 4 each have three unique identifiable mutations while rows 2 and 3 each have one known and two unknown that must be opposites. The 12 mutations at the end of the rows must be the same set of 12 at the end of the columns.

Comparing the known ones from each set leaves body circular, body square, head circular, head square unmatched from the columns and (so these must be the unknown pairs in rows 2 and 3) and biped, quadruped unmatched from the rows (so this is the unknown pair in column 2). The removing arms mutation only appears in column 1 row 1; the biped in column 2 row 1, add antennae in column 3 row 1, remove legs in column 1 row 2, add legs in column 3 row 3, remove antennae in column 1 row 4, and the add arms mutation only appears in column 3 row 4. This leaves body to circle in column 1 row 3 and head to circle in column 3 row 2. These last two are accompanied by their opposite mutations in their row so body to square is at column 2 row 3 and head to square is in column 2 row 2.

Identity Parade

Doubtful Des mugged the vicar. The correct number of liars should yield only one culprit. Suppose Shifty Sid is the villain. Then there was only one liar, the third witness. If Creepy Chris is the culprit, then there was also only one liar: the first witness. Finally, if Doubtful Des is the mugger then all three are lying. If there had been only one liar, the identity of the culprit would have been ambiguous, so there must have been three liars, with Doubtful Des being the guilty party.

Silly Pets

	Given Name	Surname	Pet
1	Mollusk	Dollup	skunk
2	Twiggle	Chump	rhinoceros
3	Polyp	Sneezer	earwig

From (2), Twiggle must have a rhinoceros. Consider each possible position of Twiggle 1, 2, or 3. If Twiggle is at 1, Polyp is at 2 and Mollusk at 3 (since only one in each column is originally correct). Also rhinoceros is at 1, earwig at 2, and skunk at 3. In this case, the relation (3) cannot fit. If Twiggle is at 3, then Polyp is at 1 and Mollusk at 2. Also following (2), rhinoceros is at 3, earwig at 1, and skunk at 2. Here, the relation (1) cannot fit. So Twiggle is at 2 (with rhinoceros). So Polyp is at 3, Mollusk at 1 and in the Pet column skunk is at 1 and earwig at 3. From (1), Chump or Sneezer is at 2, and from (3), Chump or Dollup is at 2 so Chump must be at 2. So Sneezer is at 3 and Dollup at 1.

Being Arkward

The cat was right, with the order rhinoceros, iguana, giraffe, horse, and tiger. Using initial letters and taking Noah's and the pig's "newt" statement we have R-GON, ONR-G, RONG- or -RONG. Since the wallaby can't be next to the giraffe, the W can only appear in WRONG. Taking Noah's statement and both of the cat's two statements, we have RIGH-, R-IGH, and -RIGH. The T can only fit in RIGHT. Since the puzzle asks for the "right" order, the cat's statement is the correct one.

The Boxing Match

Brutal Ben won and the punches were right jab (Ben), left to the body (Fred), right hook (Fred), left uppercut (Ben), right uppercut (Fred), right to the body (Ben), left jab (Fred), left hook (Ben). From (1) and (2), the fourth punch in (3) is neither FLJ (Fred's left jab) nor FRH since neither BLU nor BRJ are consistent with (3). So it must be either FRU or FLB. Suppose the fourth place in (3) is FLB. Then the first in (3) is either FLJ or FRH; it can't be FRU due to (4). If it is FLJ, then from (1), BLU is three places before the first in (3). From (4), FRU can either occupy the place before the first in (3) or occupies the second place in (3). In both cases, both (2) and (5) cannot fit. If the first in (3) is FRH, then from (2), BRJ is two places before the first in (3). From (1), BLU either occupies the third place in (3) with FLJ two places after the fourth in (3), or is two spaces ahead of BRJ with FLJ just after BLJ; however, in both cases, (4) and (5) cannot fit. So the fourth in (3) is not FLB as supposed and can only be FRU. From (4), BLH is three places after FRU. The first place in (3) cannot be FLJ nor FRH since from (1) and (2), more than eight places are necessary. So it must be FLB. From (1), the second place in (3) cannot be FLJ since again more than eight places occur, so it must be FRH. From (2), BRJ is one place before the first in (3). From (1), to preserve eight places, BLU must be the third place in (3) with FLJ two places after the fourth in (3). This leaves BRB one place after the fourth, satisfying (5).

Knot's Nightmare

	Groom	Bride	Honeymoon
1	alligator	fly	boots
2	cabbage	gorilla	keyhole
3	banana	egg	lake
4	duck	pizza	inkwell

From (2), pizza is at 3 or 4. If it is at 3, then from (3), gorilla is at 4. However, then no item in the second column can be correct, so pizza must be at 4 (with cabbage at 2). This means that either gorilla at 1 or egg at 3 is correct in the second column. If it is gorilla at 1, then with cabbage at 2, condition (4) cannot fit. So egg is correct at 3. Gorilla, being wrong at 1 must be at 2, with fly at 1. From (1) and (4), keyhole must be at 2. In the third column, either inkwell at 1 or lake at 3 is correct. If inkwell is correct at 1, lake must be wrong at 3 and must be at 4 with boots at 3. In that case, though, contrary to (4), both gorilla and pizza are keyhole or lake (only one of them should be). So lake is correct at 3, inkwell is wrong at 1 so must be at 4 with boots at 1. From (4), alligator or banana must be at 3. But it can't be alligator, because then both alligator and cabbage would be correct, so it's banana. Duck is wrong at 1 so must be at 4, leaving Alligator at 1.

Man of Letters

Barbara the giraffe, Gerald the leopard, Harold the gorilla, Larry the monkey and Lucy the lynx. From (2), two animals have exactly one "r" in their name and one "r" in their species. Only Gerald and Harold have just one "r" in their names, so they are those two animals. Neither of them is a monkey, then (since the word "monkey" has no "r" in it), so neither of them is one of the animals mentioned in (3). Neither is Larry, since none of the animals have 5-letter names. So that means Lucy and Barbara must be the two animals in (3). Lucy is therefore the lynx, and thus she is also the animal mentioned in (1). Barbara is either the giraffe, leopard or gorilla. As neither Gerald, Harold nor Barbara is the monkey, Larry is, and is one of the two animals mentioned in (4). Gerald cannot be the giraffe or gorilla because the animal in (1) is already accounted for, so he is the leopard. He, then, is the other animal in (4), so Barbara cannot be the gorilla and is the giraffe, leaving Harold as the gorilla.

Consequences

	Male	Female	Location	Action
1	Henry	Polly	lake	sneezed
2	Quentin	Coriander	field	argued
3	Spike	Bonny	bridge	danced
4	Butch	Tania	river	cried
5	Norman	Sylvia	shop	laughed
6	Monty	Daisy	cinema	whistled

From (6), Polly can be at 1, 2 or 3. If she is at 3 (with argued at 4 and river at 6), then from (3), Coriander can be at 1 or 2. Suppose Coriander is at 1 (with Spike at 2 and Shop at 4). Then from (6), Norman can be at 4 or 5. However, if he is at 4, then from (2), Monty cannot fit, and Norman at 5 gives both Spike and Norman correct. Suppose Coriander is at 2 (with Spike at 3 and shop at 5). From (5), Norman can be at 4 or 5. If Norman is at 4, then from (2), Monty cannot fit, and if Norman is at 5 (with whistled at 6) then both argued and whistled are correct. We conclude that Polly is not at 3. Suppose Polly is at 2 (argued at 3 and river at 5) then from

(3), Coriander is at 1 or 3. If she is at 1 (with shop at 4) both shop and river are correct. If Coriander is at 3 (with Spike at 4), then from (6), Norman can be at 3 or 5, but in neither case can (4) be true. This means that Polly is not at 2 and can only be at 1 (with argued at 2 and river at 4). From (3), Coriander can be at 2 or 3. If she is at 3, both Polly and Coriander are correct, so Coriander is at 2 (with Spike at 3 and shop at 5). From (6), Norman can be at 4 or 5, but 4 contradicts (4), so Norman is at 5 (with bridge at 3 and whistled at 6). From (1), Quentin is at 2 or 4. At 4, he and Norman are both correct, so Quentin is at 2 and Bonny at 3. From (2), Monty can only be at 6 with Tania at 4 and laughed at 5. So in the Male column, Butch is wrong at 1 so must be at 4 with Henry at 1. In the Female column, Polly is correct at 1, Daisy is wrong at 5 so must be at 6 with Sylvia at 5. In the Location column, from (5), field can only be at 2 with sneezed at 1 (in the Action column). So for location, cinema at 6 is the only one that could be correct with lake at 1. Finally, in the Action column, whistled is correct at 6, so cried must be at 4 with danced at 3.

Cards in the Cave

First Definitely Disunited, second Pity City, and third Runaround Rovers. Consider the positional statements. If we have green true (T) and red T, then blue must be false (F), or else no card could have two false statements. Then red T is first and green T must be next to blue's false positional statement, which contradicts green's true positional statement. If we have green T and red F, we must have green T first and red F third with blue T second to satisfy green's true statement, but that contradicts blue's true statement. If we have green F and red F, then blue must be true, or else no card could have two true statements. However, whatever position blue now has with the other two false statements, it is contradicted. This leaves green F and red T, so red T is first and if green F is to be satisfied then we have blue F. The red card, then, is the one with two true statements. If blue's team statement is true, then blue is Definitely Disunited, making green's team statement true as well. But that means no card has two false statements, so blue's team statement is false and green's is true, meaning red is Definitely Disunited (in first place). Runaround Rovers isn't second, so is third, and Pity City is second. (It can't be determined which team is written on the blue and green cards.)

Colored Cardigans

Blobby has yellow, Deborah has orange, Eve has blue, Flash has red and Sly has mauve. Assume that Deborah has mauve. Then neither Eve nor Sly have mauve; however, no further deductions are possible. Assume Eve has mauve. Then neither Deborah nor Sly have mauve, hence Deborah has orange, so neither Flash nor Blobby have orange, leaving Blobby with yellow. This means neither Flash nor Sly have yellow but no further deductions are possible. Assuming that Sly has mauve means as Sly doesn't have red, Flash must. Deborah doesn't have mauve, so she has orange. This leaves Eve with blue, and Blobby with yellow.

Rollerblading

Only Andy and Babs can be guaranteed to be trustworthy. Andy and Eddie have contradictory statements so either A(T)E(F) or A(F)E(T) where the letter outside the parentheses is the initial and the following letter in the parentheses represents true (T) or false (F). Babs's statement is true if Eddie lies and false otherwise, so we have A(T)B(T)E(F) or A(F)B(F)E(T). If Danny is telling the truth then Connie lies, and vice versa, so either C(F)D(T) or C(T)D(F). Connie's statement, that exactly two of the others lie, does not fit with the A(F)B(F)E(T) alternative since if it's true then three others lie, and if it's false then it contradicts the fact that there are exactly two others lying. It does fit with A(T)B(T)E(F), whether we have C(F)D(T) or C(T)D(F), so we can be sure that both Andy and Babs are truthful. The status of the Connie and Danny statements is not ascertainable.

Nightmare Neighbors

	Guy	Gal	Street
1	Colin Names	Jill Ted	Potty Place
2	Ed Ache	Anne Tagonise	Weelbee Avenue
3	Dodgy Dave	Big Bertha	Stubble Street
4	Arthur Brain	Tina Trumpet	Retch Road

From (2) and (3), Stubble Street is at 3, and from (2), only Weelbee Avenue can be at 2. So Retch Road is correct at 4, and Potty Place is at 1. Similarly, from (2), Ed Ache is at 2, and from (3), only Dodgy Dave is possible at 3. So Colin Names is at 1, leaving Arthur Brain at 4. From (3), since Tina Trumpet or Big Bertha is at 3 with Stubble Street, then the woman in (1) cannot be at 3 and can only be at 1 with Potty Place. Tina Trumpet can be at 2, 3 or 4. If Tina Trumpet is at 2, then from (3), Big Bertha is at 3. However, no item can now be correct in the second column (invalid). If she is at 3, Big Bertha can be at 2 or 4. At 2, no item can be correct in the second column (invalid). At 4, Anne Tagonise must be at 2, leaving Jill Ted at 1. However, both Anne Tagonise and Big Bertha are correct (invalid). So Tina Trumpet is at 4, Big Bertha at 3, Anne Tagonise at 2, leaving Jill Ted at 1.

Fantasy Fortune

He takes 5000 coins from the truthful goblin. Let the pixie, elf, goblin and dwarf be called P, E, G and D; and let P(5000) mean that the pixie has 5000 coins. If the pixie tells the truth, we can have P(0)G(5000) or P(5000)G(0). If the elf is truthful, we have P(2000)E(3000), P(3000)E(2000), P(0)E(5000) or P(5000)E(0). The goblin gives G(5000)D(2000) or G(3000)D(0). Finally, a truthful dwarf has possibilities P(2000)D(3000) or P(3000)D(2000). The pixie and elf statements are incompatible as are the pixie and dwarf, elf and goblin, and elf and dwarf. We need two truthful statements only. This is only possible with the pixie and goblin giving P(0)E(3000)G(5000)D(2000) or the goblin and dwarf with P(3000)E(0)G(5000)D(2000). Either way, the goblin is the one with 5000 coins.

The Interrogation

1	2	3	4
Drat	Bounder	Arbuthnot	Cad
cigar	cigarette	pipe	non-smoker

From (5), the cigar smoker was not at 4. From (6), the cigar smoker was at neither 2 nor 3 so must be at 1. From (5), the cigarette smoker was at 2. From (3), Arbuthnot is at 3. From (2) and (4), Cad must be at 4. From (1), the pipe smoker is at 3, and Bounder at 2. Drat, then, is at 1 and the non-smoker at 4.

Wildwood Grubs

1	2	3	4
Angry Alan	Desperate Dave	Brutal Bill	Cruel Colin
burglar	poisoner	strangler	knifeman

From (1), neither Bill nor Colin are in cell 2. From (5), they must be in 3/4 or 4/3, respectively, and may be eliminated from 1 while Alan and Dave can be eliminated from both 3 and 4. Condition (4) informs us that neither the burglar nor the poisoner are in 4. From (6), the strangler is not at 1 and cannot be at 4, since either Bill or Colin is at 3, so the knifeman is in 4. From (3), Colin is the knifeman in 4 and Bill is in 3. From (2), we can only have burglar, poisoner, strangler in 1, 2, 3, respectively. From (6), Dave is in 2, so Alan is in 1.

Order in Class

Peter was sitting in the center row of the first column and the class was studying COMPUTING (found by taking the first letter of each name in the solution, back to front, in sequence).

Colin	Oliver	Maggie
Peter	Ursula	Tina
Ivan	Norman	George

If we number the squares 1–9 from left to right along the rows starting with the back row then the second sentence means that either Ursula is 5 and George 9 or Ursula is 4 and George 8. Since Ivan and George share the same row, Colin and Maggie cannot be at 7 and 9. If Ursula is at 4, Colin must be at 1 which does not allow Oliver to be above Ursula. So Ursula is at 5 with George at 9 and Oliver at 2. Norman and Tina can only now be at 8 and 6, respectively, giving Colin at 1 and Maggie at 3. Ivan is then at 7 so Peter is at 4.

Circle of Cons

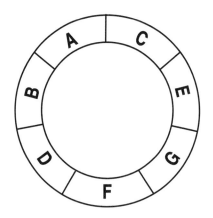

Andy must be next to Bill and Fred is next to George. Reading clockwise, taking the relationship between Ernie and Fred allows E-FG, FGE, GF-E or EGF. Adding the relationship between Dave and Ernie gives the possibilities E-FGD, DFGE, D-FGE, DGF-E, EGFD or EFG-D. The relationship between Colin and Dave eliminates two of those, giving ECFGD, DFGEC, DGFCE or CEGFD. Finally, the relationship between Andy, Bill and Colin allows ABECFGD, ABDFGEC, DGFCEBA or CEGFDBA. Testing each of these against the given order in their seven possible rotated positions shows that only the above solution exists.

Strange Signs

Sign B has three correct, C has two correct, D has one correct and A has none. Note the symmetry of the square; for example, the distance from B to C is the distance from C to B.

Suppose row A has three correct numbers. Then 19 in row B is wrong, 19 in row C is correct and 17 in row D is correct. The correct position of the 19 being found, it is therefore wrong in row D. We now know that row B must be the one that is completely wrong. So 18 in row C is incorrect. The 20s in rows C and D are both incorrect because the 20 is correct in row A, and no distances are repeated.

Assuming row C has three correct numbers means that 19 in row A, 18 in row B, and 20 in row D are correct and no row can have none correct (invalid).

If row D has three correct, the 17 in A and the 20 in C are correct while the 15 in B is not. Nonrepeatability means that the 19s in rows A, B and C are wrong. Only row B can have all numbers wrong but if 18 is wrong then so is 18 in row C. The 20 is wrong in A (since it is the distance from C to D) and no row has exactly two correct.

Finally, if row B has three correct, the 20 is wrong in A, 18 is correct in C, and all other 19s are wrong (nonrepeatability). If the 17s are now correct, no row has none correct so they must be wrong. The remaining two 20s are correct to get the right combination of correct distances.

Fair's Fair

There were three balls under each and the third statement was true. If only one statement is true, that statement must be the only one to have the correct number. The numbers one, two and four appear in more than one statement. The number three appears in only the third statement and so that must be the true one.

Logic Letters

The writer is John GALSWORTHY, author of *The Forsyte Saga* novels and a Nobel prizewinner in literature in 1932. The solution arises from the choices GA(2), LS(3), WO(4), RT(5), HY(6).

Party Puzzle

Fred	Blue	Leather
Jim	Yellow	Cotton
Sally	Red	Wool

From (2) and (3), the person in cotton was also in yellow and, from (4), was Jim or Fred. Using (1), Sally must have wool. From (5), since Sally is in neither yellow nor blue, she must have red. Using (6), Fred must now be in blue and leather, leaving Jim in yellow and cotton.

Breakfast on the Farm

cow	cornflakes	barn
goat	porridge	field
horse	grits	shed
pig	toast	house

From (5) and (7), the pig must eat in the barn or the house. From (3), if it eats in the barn, it must eat cornflakes or porridge which is invalid from (2) and (7). So the pig eats in the house. From (1), the horse eats in the shed. Using (2) and (7), the pig can eat toast or grits, but from (6), grits is eliminated, so the pig eats toast in the house. From (4) and (6), the horse must eat the grits in the shed. Using (2), the cow eats cornflakes in the barn so the goat eats porridge in the field.

Mad Nomads

Carrie had the rent. Denzil occupied front left, Barbara front right, Arnie back left and Carrie back right. Take the first letters of the names and let the order denote the room positions from left to right starting at the front (e.g., BCAD means B front left, C front right, A back left, D back right). Now, if exactly two statements are true, then the correct arrangement must have two and only two statements that refer to the same room (and those two statements are the true ones). Suppose A is fixed. Then we can have (a) ACDB or (b) ADBC. In (a), A, B, and D's statements refer to the same room, which is too many. In (b) no statements refer to the same room. Suppose C is fixed. Then we have BDCA or DACB. In both cases, no statements refer to the same room. Suppose D is fixed. Then we can have CABD or BCAD. Again, in both cases no statements refer to the same room. If B is fixed, we have (a) CBDA or (b) DBAC. In (a), no two statements refer to the same room, but in (b), A and D both refer to the back right room, which is Carrie's, and so theirs must be the true statements and DBAC the correct arrangement.

Spy of the Year

	First Name	Surname	Code Name
1	Hans	Anfit	Tikelikov
2	Nick	Errs	Hadenov
3	Choo	Hing	Nodapov
4	Baz	Teale	Fingsarov

From (1), (4) and (5), Nick can only be at 2 with Hing at 3. So from (2) and (3), Teale is at 4 and Nodapov at 3. In the first column, we know Nick is at 2, so Choo and Nick are wrongly positioned and from (5) Hans is not at 3. So Baz is the only one correct at 4. With Nick at 2, Hans can only be at 1 with Choo at 3. For the second column, we know Teale is correct at 4 with the others wrong. We already know Hing is at 3 so Anfit can only be at 1 with Errs at 2. In the third column, we know Nodapov is correct at 3 and the rest wrong. From (3), Fingsarov is not at 1 so can only be at 4. So Hadenov is at 2 and Tikelicov at 1.

The Four Cats

Ginger ate rabbit, Pickle ate salmon, Sooty ate chicken and Tigger ate turkey. If the lamb is eaten we must have turkey next to it, which in turn necessitates chicken next to that, in the order CTL (LTC can't be right because turkey must be to the right of chicken). This means only salmon could be the fourth food because rabbit necessitates salmon also. So one possible set of combinations is CTLS or SCTL. Without lamb, we can have the other four without requiring lamb, allowing the combinations CTRS, CTSR, RSCT or SRCT (with turkey adjacent to chicken but to its right, and rabbit adjacent to salmon). Ginger dislikes chicken, so all combinations with chicken in the first bowl can be eliminated, leaving SCTL, RSCT and SRCT. Pickle, who has the second bowl, hates rabbit, so SRCT isn't correct. Tigger, who has the last bowl, hates lamb, so SCTL isn't correct, leaving RSCT as the only possible combination.

Real Ale Contest

	First Name	Surname	Country
1	Denise	Hogwash	Lithuania
2	Ben	Guzzle	Ireland
3	Colin	Earwig	Jamaica
4	Agatha	Flop	Kenya

From (2) and (3), Ben cannot at 1 because of the restriction on Jamaica and cannot be at 4 since he is above Jamaica. So Ben is at 2 or 3. If Ben is at 3 (with Jamaica at 4), from (4), Colin can be at 1 or 2. At 1, both Colin and Ben are correct (invalid). At 2 (with Flop at 3), from (1), Guzzle can be at 2 or 4. At 2 (with Lithuania at 1), there can be none correct in the third column (invalid). At 4, both Flop and Guzzle are correct in the second column (invalid). So Ben is not at 3 and must be at 2 (with Jamaica at 3). From (1), Lithuania is at 1 or 2. At 2, both Lithuania and Jamaica are correct (invalid). So Lithuania is at 1 (with Guzzle at 2). From (4), Colin can only fit at 3 (with Flop at 4). In the first column, only Agatha can be correct at 4 so Denise is at 1. For the second column, only Hogwash can be correct at 1 so Earwig is at 3. In the third column, Jamaica is correct at 3, Ireland is wrong at 4 so must be at 2 with Kenya at 4.

Resort to Reason

	1	2	3	4
Landlord	C	D	B	A
Guest	F	G	E	H
Guesthouse	K	I	L	J

From conditions (1), (2), and (5), we either have (a) Harry at 1, Bob at 2, and Kestrelview at 4; or (b) Kestrelview at 1, Bob at 3, and Harry at 4. From (2), Ivorytowers must be at 2 or 3, so from (4) and (6) we have either (c) Arthur at 1, Eunice at 2, and Ivorytowers at 3; or (d) Ivorytowers at 2, Eunice at 3, and Arthur at 4. For the combinations (a)(c), (a)(d), and (b)(c), there's nowhere that (3) can fit, so (b)(d) is the correct combination, and Frances is at 1, Daniel at 2, and Lavender at 3, which leaves Colin at 1, Geraldine at 2, and Jollyjapes at 4.

Hogweed's Pond

	Creature	Home	Rise Time	Cereal
1	frog	reeds	7 a.m.	Lice Krispies
2	otter	boot	9 a.m.	Pondpops
3	newt	hollow log	10 a.m.	Flyflakes
4	toad	sticks	8 a.m.	Waterbix
5	perch	dam	6 a.m.	Codflakes

From (1) and (6), the Lice Krispies diner can only be at 1 or 2. If it is at 2, using (1) and (7), the Flyflakes diner can only be at 3. This gives two correct in the Cereal column (invalid), so the Lice Krispies diner is at 1 (with the newt at 3). Then, using (4) and (5), the 10 a.m. riser can only be at 3 and so, using (2) and (8), the 9 a.m. riser can only be at (2) with the reeds dweller at 1. Using (7), the Flyflakes eater is then at 2 or 3. If it is at 2 (with the dam resident at 4), that gives both dam and reeds correct in the House column (invalid), so Flyflakes is not at 2 and must be at 3 with dam at 5. So the newt is correctly positioned in the Creature column, reeds in the House column, 10 a.m. in the Rise time column, and Flyflakes in the Cereal column.

In the Creature column, the perch is wrong at 4, cannot be at 2 due to (5), so must be at 5. The toad is wrong at 2, so must be at 4 leaving the otter at 2. In the House column, sticks is incorrect at 2, cannot be at 3 due to (1), so must be at 4. The boot is wrong at 3, so must be at 2 leaving the hollow log at 3. For the Rising time, 6 a.m. is wrong at 1, is not at 4 due to (8), so must be at 5. The 7 a.m. time is incorrect at 4, so must be at 1. So 8 a.m. is at 4. The Cereal column has Pondpops incorrect at 4, it cannot be at 5 due to (3), so must be at 2. Waterbix is wrong at 5, so is at 4. So Codflakes is at 5.

34. Changing Words

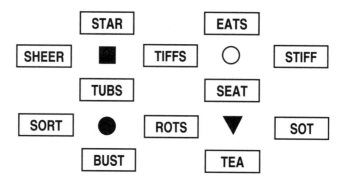

The black square advances each letter one forward in the alphabet, the white circle moves the last letter to the front, the black circle changes the letter order to 3, 2, 4, 1, and the triangle removes the first letter and moves the last to the front.

Insects Incorporated

	Applicant	Previous Job	Intended Position
1	cockroach	kleptomaniac	security guard
2	beetle	detective	receptionist
3	ant	priest	manager
4	millipede	gravedigger	treasurer

From (2) and (4), the ant can be at 2 or 3. If the ant is at 2, from (1) and (3), the beetle must be at 4 (with the security guard at 3) and so, from (5), the detective can only be at 1 (with the manager at 2). However, this gives both the manager and security guard correctly positioned in the intended position column (invalid). So the ant is not at 2 and is at 3 (with the gravedigger at 4). Then from (3), the beetle can be at 2 or 4. If the beetle is at 4 then both the beetle and ant are correct in the first column (invalid). So the beetle is at 2 (with the security guard at 1), then from (5), the detective can be at 1, 2 or 3. With the detective at 1, together with the gravedigger at 4, there are two correct in the Previous job column (invalid). If the detective is at 3 (with the manager at 4) then none can be correct in the Intended Position column. So the detective is at 2 (with the manager at 3). In the first column, the ant is correct at 3, the millipede is wrong at 1 so can only be at 4 with the cockroach at 1. For the second column, the gravedigger is correct at 4, the kleptomaniac is wrong at 3 so must be at 1 with the priest at 3. Finally, in the third column, only the treasurer can be correct at 4, so the receptionist is at 2.

Puzzle in the Park

	Squirrel	Tree	Nuts
1	Scamper	Oak	10
2	Tufty	Birch	11
3	Basil	Ash	12
4	Gerald	Sycamore	9

Using (3), Scamper can be at 1 or 2. If it is at 2, then from (2), Tufty can be at 3 or 4. He cannot be at 3 because then 10 nuts would be at 2, which contradicts (4), and if Tufty is at 4, then both Tufty and Scamper are correct (invalid). So Scamper must be at 1 (with the ash at 3). From (1), the sycamore cannot be at 2 since this gives both the sycamore and the ash correct (invalid). So the sycamore must be at 4 (with 12 nuts at 3). Using (2), the 10 nuts cannot be at 2 because of (4), so must be at 1 (with Tufty at 2).

We now know that only Basil can be correct in the Squirrel column at 2 and Gerald must be at 4. The correct tree is the ash at 3, so the birch must be at 2 with the oak at 1. For the number of nuts, only 9 nuts can be correctly positioned at 4, so 11 nuts is at 2.

Murder at Little Winkle

The person who committed the murder was Jim the geologist. We have 3 p.m., Jim the geologist; 5 p.m., Sid the lawyer; 8 p.m., Alice the pharmacist; and 9 p.m., Connie the grocer. The 3 p.m. statement reveals that neither Jim nor Alice is a lawyer or a grocer, and therefore neither Connie nor Sid is the geologist or pharmacist. The 5 p.m. statement gives Connie as the grocer, so Sid as the lawyer. Also, the 5 p.m. speaker is neither Connie nor Jim. If Jim is not the pharmacist, then the pharmacist must be Alice with Jim as the geologist. Since the speaker is not a pharmacist, the speaker is also not Alice, and must be Sid. From the 8 p.m. statement, that speaker is not Jim. From the 9 p.m. statement, the speaker is neither Alice nor Jim so must be Connie. It follows that the 8 p.m. suspect is Alice the pharmacist and the 3 p.m. one is Jim the geologist. If the watch stopped at 20:51 only Alice the pharmacist could have done it. However, closer inspection of the drawing of the watch will reveal that the digital "1" is written to the left of its space instead of the right and so the drawing was made upside down. This gives the actual time as 15:02, allowing only Jim the geologist the chance to do it.

Bank on Us

	Bank	Manager	Street
1	Badmove	Mr. Tremble	Trumpet
2	Hirate	Ms. Manidge	Daisy
3	Rippemov	Mr. Fortune	Porcupine
4	Savehup	Mrs. Chance	Arlington

Using (3) and (5), the Mr. Tremble can be at 1 or 3. If he is at 3 (with the Hirate bank at 4), then using (4), the Rippemov bank can be at 2 or 3. If it is at 2, then both the Rippemov bank and the Hirate bank are correct (invalid). If it is at 3, then the Hirate bank is correctly positioned and the Badmove bank must be at 2 contradicting (1). So Mr. Tremble can only be at 1 (with the Hirate bank at 2). Then using (2), Ms. Manidge is at 2 or 3. If she is at 3, then both she and Mr. Tremble are correct (invalid). So Ms. Manidge is at 2 (with Porcupine Street at 3). From (4), the Rippemov bank can only be at 3 (with Daisy Street at 2). For the Bank column, only the Badmove bank can be correct at 1 so the Savehup bank is at 4. Mr. Tremble is correctly positioned at 1 in the Manager column, so Mr. Fortune must be at 3 and Mrs. Chance at 4. In the Street column, Porcupine Street must be correct at 3, Trumpet Street is wrong at 4 and so must be at 1, and Arlington Street is at 4.

Tape Teaser

	Nickname	Surname	Hometown
1	Sugar	Holyhead	Boston
2	Rocky	Freeman	New York
3	Basher	McCool	Seattle
4	Iron	Tryson	Texas

Using (3), Sugar can be at 1 or 2. If he is at 2 (with McCool at 4), then using (2), Iron can be at 3 or 4. If Iron is at 4, both he and Sugar are correctly positioned (invalid). If he is at 3 (with Seattle at 2), then using (1), Boston can only be at 1 giving both Boston and Seattle correctly positioned (invalid). So Sugar is not at 2 and must be at 1. From (1), Freeman can be at 2 or 4. However, with Freeman at 4, both Freeman and McCool are correct (invalid). So Freeman is at 2, and Boston is at 1. Using (2), Seattle can now be at 2 or 3. If it is at 2, both Boston and Seattle are correct (invalid). So Seattle is at 3 (with Iron at 4). For the Nickname column, only Basher at 3 can can be correct so Rocky is at 2. In the Surname column, McCool is correct at 3, Tryson is wrong at 1 so must be at 4 with Holyhead at 1. The correct Hometown is Boston at 1; New York is therefore wrong at 4 and can only be at 2 with Texas at 4.

The Greatest Human Being

	First Name	Surname	Specialty
1	Charles	Newtune	Cleaner
2	Albert	Darling	Welder
3	Isaac	Eyeline	Gardener
4	Marie	Curious	Bricklayer

Using (1), Albert is at 1 or 2. If he is at 1, then from (2), Charles is at 2 or 3. However, with Charles at 2 (and Darling at 3), from (3), Curious can only be at 4 and so it is not possible to find just one correct entry in the Surname column (Newtune and Eyeline must be both correct or both incorrect). If Charles is at 3 (with Darling at 4), then from (3), Curious can only be at 3. This gives both Curious and Darling correct (invalid). So Albert is not at 1 and must be at 2 (with the bricklayer at 4).

From (2), Charles can be at 1 or 3. However, if Charles is at 3 (with Darling at 4), then from (3), Curious can only be at 3, and so both Curious and Darling are correct (invalid). So Charles is at 1 (with Darling at 2). From (3), Curious can now be at 3 or 4, but if Curious is at 3 (with the welder at 1) then both the welder and bricklayer are correct (invalid). This gives Curious at 4 (with the welder at 2). For the First Name, Albert is correct at 2, Marie is wrong at 3 and can only be at 4 and so Isaac is at 3. In the Surname column, only Newtune can be correct at 1, so Eyeline is at 3. The bricklayer must be the correct specialty at 4, the cleaner can only be at 1 and so the gardener is at 3.

The Feed-'em-Fat Diner

	First Name	Surname	Occupation
1	Dave	Gateau	waiter
2	Bill	Jaffa	receptionist
3	Anne	Ingest	manager
4	Connie	Fish	dishwasher
5	Eleanor	Haddock	chef

From (4), Eleanor is at 4 or 5. Suppose Eleanor is at 4, with the receptionist at 1. Then from (3), Anne can only be at 5, making both Eleanor and Anne correct (invalid). So Eleanor is at 5 (with the receptionist at 2). Using (1), the manager is at 1 or 3. If he is at 1, both the manager and the receptionist are correct (invalid), so he must be at 3 (with Haddock at 5). From (2), Ingest can be at 3 or 4. However, if Ingest is at 4, both Ingest and Haddock are correct (invalid), so Ingest must be at 3 (with Dave at 1). Using (3), the waiter can only be at 1 (with Anne at 3). In the first name column, Dave is correct at 1, Connie is wrong at 2 and can only be at 4 so Bill is at 2. For the surname, Haddock is correct at 5, Fish is wrong at 2, cannot be at 1 due to (5), so must be at 4. So Jaffa, who is wrong at 1 must be at 2 and Gateau at 1. In the occupation column, the receptionist is correct at 2, the dishwasher is wrong at 5 so must be at 4. This leaves the chef at 5.

Snow White

Dopey's pseudonym was Celia. Since Ernie is immediately in front of Andrea, the Florence/Ernie and Andrea/Brian relations can either be F — E A – – B, F B – E A – F B, or B— E A – F. Only in the last of these is Brian ahead of Florence. The Henry/Celia relation puts the Gertie/Henry relation in front of the block so that the Celia/Daniel relation fills the gaps in the block. This gives the order as Gertie, Henry, Brian, Celia, Ernie, Andrea, Daniel, Florence.

Pet Places

	Pet	Street 1	Street 2
1	dog	Rubble	Lane
2	elephant	Hollow	Avenue
3	alligator	Purple	Crescent
4	parakeet	Apple	Drive
5	cat	Grunter	Road
6	frog	Tempest	Walk

From (6), Hollow can be at 1 or 2. If it is at 1 (with the frog at 5 and Crescent at 2), from (1), Rubble can only fit at 2 (with the alligator at 4 and Drive at 5). Using (2) and (3), Purple can only be at 4 but this means that both the dog and alligator are correct (invalid). So Hollow is not at 1 and must be at 2 (with Crescent at 3 and the frog at 6). From (1), Rubble can be at 1 or 3. If it is at 3, both Hollow and Rubble are correct (invalid). So Rubble is at 1 (with the alligator at 3 and Drive at 4). Using (3) and (4), Avenue can only be at 2 (with Purple at 3 and the dog at 1). For the Pet column, the frog is correct at 6, the parakeet is wrong at 5, cannot be at 2 due to (5) so must be at 4. The cat cannot be at 2 due to (5) so must appear at 5 with the elephant at 2. The Street 1 column has Hollow correct at 2. Tempest is wrong at 4, cannot be at 5 due to (2), so must be at 6. Apple, being wrong at 5, can only be at 4 with Grunter at 5. In the Street 2 column, Crescent is correct at 3. Lane is wrong at 6, cannot be at 5 due to (4), so must be at 1. Walk is wrong at 5 so must be at 6 with Road at 5.

The Show Must Go On

	Play	Company	Location
1	Hamlet	Amnesiacs	Sydney
2	Othello	Egomaniacs	London
3	Macbeth	Lovelies	Ontario
4	Julius Caesar	Ditherers	New York

From (4), Sydney can only be at 1 or 2. If it is at 2 (with the Lovelies at 4), then from (2), Hamlet can be at 1 or 2. However, if it is at 1 (with the Egomaniacs at 2), both the Lovelies and Egomaniacs are correct (invalid). Hamlet at 2 (with the Egomaniacs at 3), means that from (1), Julius Caesar can only be at 4, and so no entry in the first column can be correct (invalid). So Sydney is not at 2 and must be at 1 (with the Lovelies at 3). Hamlet can now only be at 1 or 3. If it is at 3, the Egomaniacs must be at 4 contradicting (3). So Hamlet is at 1 (with the Egomaniacs at 2). Ontario can now be at either 2 or 3. If it is at 2 (with Julius Caesar at 3), both Hamlet and Julius Caesar are correct (invalid). So Ontario is at 3 (with Julius Caesar at 4). This gives Hamlet correct in the Play column; Macbeth is wrong at 2 so must be at 3 with Othello at 2. In the Company column, the Egomaniacs are correct, the Ditherers are wrong at 1 so must be at 4 with the Amnesiacs at 1. For the Location column, Ontario is right, New York is wrong at 2 so must be at 4 with London at 2.

Prime Time

	Performer	Action	Adverb
1	wife	laughing	softly
2	dog	whistling	unashamedly
3	cat	tapping	loudly
4	pig	belching	aggressively
5	neighbor	sneezing	timidly

From (6), softly can be at 1 or 2. Suppose it is at 2 (with pig at 5). Then from (3), neighbor can be at 3 or 4. If neighbor is at 3 (with tapping at 1), from (1), laughing can be at 2 or 3. If it is at 2, then both tapping and laughing are correct (invalid). If it is at 3 (with loudly at 5), then (4) is violated. If instead, Neighbor is at 4, then both Pig and Neighbor are correct (invalid). So softly is not at 2. With softly at 1 (so that pig is at 4), from (3), neighbor can be at 3 or 5. If it is at 3 (with tapping at 1), from (1), laughing can be at 2 or 3. At 2, both tapping and laughing are correct (invalid). If it is at 3 (with loudly at 5), then from (5), cat can only be at 2 so that sneezing is at 4 violating (2). So Neighbor is at 5 (with tapping at 3). Then, from (1), laughing can be at 1 or 2. If laughing is at 2 (with loudly at 4), then with Softly at 1 and loudly at 4, condition (4) is violated. This means that laughing can only be at 1 (with loudly at 3). From (5), cat can be at 2 or 3. If it is at 2 so that sneezing is at 4 then (2) is violated. So cat must be at 3 (with sneezing at 5). This gives the correct items in each column as cat, sneezing and softly. In the Performer column, since dog is wrong at 1, it can only be at 2, so that wife is at 1. For Action, whistling must be wrong at 4 and can only be at 2, so that belching is at 4. In the Adverb column, unashamedly is wrong at 5, cannot be at 4 due to (2), so must be at 2. Timidly is wrong at 4 so can only be at 5 with aggressively at 4.

The Dragemround Dance

	Male First Name	Male Surname	Female First Name	Female Surname
1	Alan	Kerr	Marie	Kinnear
2	Rob	Teef	Anne	Teak
3	Buck	Foulkes	Olive	Dunn
4	Joe	Drover	Emma	Ulman

From (1), Rob can be at 2 or 3. If he is at 3 (with Marie at 2 and Foulkes at 4), then from (3), Buck can only be at 4 (with Kerr at 2 and Teak at 3). This gives both Buck and Rob correct (invalid). If Rob is at 2 (with Marie at 1 and Foulkes at 3), and from (3), Buck can be at 3 or 4. If Buck is at 4 (with Kerr at 2 and Teak at 3), then both Kerr and Foulkes are correct (invalid). So Buck is at 3 (with Kerr at 1 and Teak at 2). From (2), Kinnear can only be at 1 (with Olive at 3). For the male first name, only Alan can be correct at 1, so Joe is at 4. The male surname has Foulkes correct at 3, Teef must be wrong at 4 so is at 2 and Drover is at 4. For the female first name, Olive is correct at 3, Emma is wrong at 2 so must be at 4 and Anne is at 2. Finally, for the female surname, only Ulman can be correct at 4, so Dunn must be at 3.

Funny Fours

	First	Second	Third	Fourth
1	L	A	Z	Y
2	B	R	O	W
3	S	P	I	N
4	D	U	C	K
5	T	H	E	M

From (4), L can be at 1 or 2. If it is at 2 (with C at 5 and N at 4) then from (5), M can only be at 5. This gives both M and N correct for the fourth letter (invalid). So L is at 1 (with C at 4 and N at 3). From (2), K can be at 2 or 4. If it is at 2 (with I at 1 and H at 3), then from (5), M can only be at 5. This gives both K and M correct in the fourth column (invalid). So K is at 4 (with I at 3 and H at 5). From (5), M is at 5 (with O at 2) so that from (1), B is at 2 (with U at 4). Now since S is one of the last three places in the first letter column and P is one of the first three in the second letter column then from (3), both S and P are at 3. For the first column, B is correct at 2, T is wrong at 4 so must be at 5 with D at 4. In the second column, U is correct at 4, A is wrong at 2 so must be at 1 leaving R at 2. The third column has I correct at 3; E is wrong at 1 so must be at 5 with Z at 1. In the fourth column, M is correct at 5, W is wrong at 1 so must be at 2 with Y at 1.

P&B Club

The correct order was Connie, Agatha, Ethel, Bertha and Denise. Let A1 denote Agatha in position 1 and (a), (b), (c) represent the three orders mentioned. From the change from (b) to (c), either E3 or C5 is correct in (c). Assuming A1 is correct, then D2, C3, B4, E5 in (b) are all wrong. Assuming E3 is right, then C5 is wrong in (c) and B2, C4, D5 are wrong in (a). This gives A1, C2, E3, D4, B5 violating the condition that C and E are not together. Assuming C5 is right instead of E3, then D2, E3, B4 are wrong in (c) and B2 must be right in (a). This gives A1, B2, D3, E4, C5 and C and E are again wrongly together. So our assumption that A1 is correct must be wrong.

Let us assume that A1 is wrong, C5 is correct and E3

wrong so that D5 is wrong in (a) and B2 is correct. This means
there can be no correct places in (b) contrary to expectation. Let
us assume that A1 is wrong and E3 is correct. Then C3 and
E5 are wrong in (b) and either D2 or B4 is correct. Assuming
D2 is correct, then B2/D5 are wrong in (a) so C4 is correct,
violating the CE separation condition. Assuming B4 is correct
instead of D2, then C4 is wrong in (a) so D5 must be right.
We can now only have C1, A2, E3, B4, D5.

Trotter Farm

A=4, B=2, C=9, D=8, E=6, F=1, G=3, H=7, I=5. Three of A, C, E, F,
G, H are wrong. At least one of A=2 and G=3 must be wrong
otherwise D=10. Also at least one of C=9 and F=8 must be wrong
otherwise the last column total is too big. Following Snout, assume
A and C are correct then F and G are wrong and B=4. So only
one of E and H is correct. If E=5 is correct then H=6 and the
remaining numbers will not fit. If H=7 is correct then E=4 and
we have repetition. Following Curly, assume E and F are correct;
then D=2. However, A cannot be 2 (repetition) and C cannot be 9
(last column total). So just one of G or H is correct. If G=3 then
A=10 (invalid). If H=7 then B=3 and the remaining numbers cannot fit. Therefore Bacon must have made two true statements, so
G and H are both correct, giving I=5 (which means E is wrong).
If F=8 is correct then C=2. However, the remaining numbers will
not fit. So both E and F are wrong and only one of A or C is
right. If A=2 then D=10 (invalid) so C=9 is correct, F=1.

Another way to find the solution: There are only 8 number
triplets that total 15: 159, 249, 168, 258, 348, 267, 357, 456. The
triplets that do not fit in a row or column are 258 and 456 since
the digits 1, 3, 7, 9 that appear in two triplets only (corresponding
to an appearance in one row and column) necessarily qualify
those triplets and exclude the remaining two triplets. This
allows any variation of the above solution where two rows or
two columns are juxtaposed. However, certain restrictions
apply to the solution. For example, 5 and 8 cannot finish in the
same row nor column so at least one of Curly's statements is
false. At least one of A and G is false otherwise D=10 which is
invalid. The numbers 3 and 8 must be in the same row or column
as must 3, 7, 5. Checking the 12 true/false combinations of the
six statements against these conditions leads to the solution.

Whodunnit?

	First Name	Surname	Weapon	Location
1	Alice	Thrust	hammer	library
2	Lyn	Loosenut	gun	study
3	James	Nutter	poison	hall
4	Eunice	Bracket	rope	conservatory
5	Sid	Kilroy	knife	kitchen

From (5), gun can be at 1, 2 or 3. However, from (2) we immediately deduce that it cannot be at 1. If gun is at 3 (with hall at 4 and Eunice at 5), then from (1), knife can only be at 4. This gives both gun and knife correct (invalid), so gun must be at 2 (with Hall at 3 and Eunice at 4). From (1), conservatory can be at 2 or 4. If it is at 2 then both conservatory and hall are correct (invalid). So conservatory is at 4 (with Nutter at 3 and Knife at 5). From (3), Kilroy can be at 4 or 5. If it is at 4, both Nutter and Kilroy are correct (invalid) so Kilroy is at 5 (with James at 3). From (2) and (6), Alice must be at 1 (with library at 1). In the Weapon column, only hammer at 1 can be correct. From (4), poison can only be at 3 (with Bracket at 4). This leaves rope at 4. In the First name column, only Lyn can be correct at 2, so Sid is at 5. For the Surname, since Nutter is correct at 3, then Thrust is wrong at 2 so must be at 1 with Loosenut at 2. Finally, in the Location column, hall is correct at 3, study is wrong at 5 so must be at 2, leaving kitchen at 5.

Fancy Dress Party

	Name	Nickname	Costume	Beverage
1	Charles	Tubby	kangaroo	lemonade
2	Elizabeth	Nibble	tree	tea
3	William	Piggy	clown	coffee
4	Harry	Fly	alien	water

From (4), Tubby can be at 1 or 2. If Tubby is at 2, then from (1), Clown can be at 1 or 2. If it is at 1, from (6), kangaroo is at 2 or 3. If it is at 2, then (3) is violated. If it is at 3 (with Elizabeth at 4), from (2), William can be at 2 or 3. If William is at 2 (with Fly at 3), then (5) is violated. If William is at 3, both William and Elizabeth are correct (invalid). So clown is not at 1 here. If clown is at 2, from (6), kangaroo can be at 1 or 3 and in both cases (3) is violated. So Tubby must be at 1 (with coffee at 3). From (1), clown can be at 1 or 3. If it is at 1 (with water at 2) then the positions of water and coffee allow no correct entries in the Drink column (invalid). So clown is correct at 3 (with water correct at 4). From (3) and (6), kangaroo is at 1 (with Elizabeth at 2). From (2), Fly can be at 2 or 4. If Fly is at 2, condition (5) is violated. So Fly is at 4 (with William at 3). In the first column, William is correct at 3, Harry is wrong at 1 so must be at 4 with Charles at 1. In the Nickname column, Tubby is correct at 1, Piggy is wrong at 2 so must be at 3, leaving Nibble at 2. For the Costume, clown is correct at 3, tree is wrong at 4 so must be at 2, leaving alien at 4. Finally, for the Drink column, water is right at 4, lemonade is wrong at 2 so can only be at 1 with tea at 2.

Dogs of War

The question was CAN YOU BEG? From (4) and (5), Yapper and Ugly can only appear in the second row in the first and second columns, respectively. From (2) and (4), Bumchew must be top left or bottom left with Nasher in the opposite corner. From (3) and (6), Canine cannot be in the third column because there are dogs to the right of him, nor the second column because then four dogs would appear in the third column (since Nasher and Ugly are already in the third column). So Canine is in the first column top left or bottom left, with Oddear and Aggro in the second column. From (2), Evileye is also in the second column. So Growler can only be in the remaining space in the third column. From (1), Growler cannot be top right because Oddear is in the row above. So Growler is bottom right, Nasher is top right, Bumchew is bottom left, Canine top left with Aggro directly to the right. From (1), Oddear is in the center, leaving Evileye in the middle of the bottom row.

Alien Court

	Captain	Planet	Spaceship
1	Arial	Grunt	Boldleego
2	Ponga	Loopy	Supersnail
3	Tweak	Blink	Outagas
4	Bleep	Ether	Hosspuld
5	Riddle	Pobble	Rustcan

From (2), Grunt can be at 1, 2 or 3. If Grunt is at 2 (with Ponga at 3 and Outagas at 4) then condition (4) cannot fit. If Grunt is at 3 (with Ponga at 4 and Outagas at 5), then from (4), Blink can only be at 1 but then both Blink and Grunt are correct (invalid). So Grunt is at 1 (with Ponga at 2 and Outagas at 3). From (4), Blink can only fit at 3 (with Riddle at 5 and Hosspuld at 4). From (1), if Boldleego is somewhere above Pobble, then Boldleego can be at 1 or 2. If it is at 2 then both Boldleego and Hosspuld are correct (invalid). So Boldleego is at 1. This means that with Hosspuld correct in the Spaceship column, Supersnail is wrong at 5 so must be at 2, leaving Rustcan at 5. From (1), if Pobble is not above Rustcan, then Pobble must be at 5. In the Planet column, only Loopy can be correct at 2 so Ether is at 4. In the Captain column, Riddle is correct, Arial is wrong at 3, cannot be at 4 due to (3) so must be at 1. Tweak is wrong at 4 so is at 3 and Bleep is at 4.

Mixed Marriage

	Male	Female	Surname
1	Chris	Ivy	Ogden
2	Andy	Gina	Levy
3	Dan	Fiona	Marsden
4	Bob	Jill	Kennett
5	Eddie	Harriet	Norris

From (5), Ivy can be at 1, 2 or 3. If she is at 2 (with Marsden at 4), then from (2), Fiona can be at 1 or 3. Either way, condition (3) is violated. If Ivy is at 3, then Fiona is at 1 or 2. At 1,

both Fiona and Ivy are correct (invalid), and at 2, condition
(3) is violated. So Ivy must be at 1. Then from (2), Fiona can
be at 2 or 3. If Fiona is at 2, then (3) is violated. So Fiona
must be at 3 (with Eddie at 5). This means that, from (4),
Dan is at 3 (with Jill at 4 and Levy at 2). Then, from (1), Andy
is at 2 (with Kennett at 4). In the first column, Dan is correct
at 3, Bob is wrong at 1 so must be at 4 with Chris at 1. For
the second column, only Harriet can be correct at 5, so Gina
is at 2. Finally, for the third column, only Ogden can be
correct at 1 so Norris is at 5.

A Meal Out

	Nickname	Name	Food	Beverage
1	Wimpsy	Chris	beef	cappuccino
2	Bigears	Annie	chicken	tea
3	Doghouse	Steve	pork	latte
4	Tender	Georgina	lamb	mocha
5	Simple	Jackie	fish	milkshake

From (4) and (6), both Steve and Chris can be at 1, 2 or 3. To
fulfill (3), they must be at 1 and 3 in some order. If Steve is at
1 and Chris is at 3, then both are correct (invalid), So Chris is
at 1 (with Bigears at 2 and latte at 3) and Steve is at 3 (with
fish at 5 and mocha at 4). From (2), Tender can be at 3 or 4.
At 3, both Bigears and Tender are correct (invalid), so Tender
must be at 4 (with pork at 3 and tea at 2). Using (1) and (5),
Annie will only fit in at 2 (with beef at 1). In the first column,
Bigears is correct at 2, Doghouse is wrong at 1, cannot be at 5
because of condition (5), so must be at 3. Wimpsy is wrong at
5 so must be at 1 leaving Simple at 5. For the second column,
Annie is correct at 2; Jackie is therefore wrong at 4 and can
only be at 5 with Georgina at 4. Fish is the correct entry in
the third column; chicken is incorrect at 4 so must be at 2
with lamb at 4. In the fourth column, mocha is correct at 4;
milkshake is therefore wrong at 1 and must be at 5, leaving
cappuccino at 1.

Whose Pet Is It?

Anita has the parrot, Ben the fish, Chuck the parakeet, Debbie the owl, Eliza the dog, and Fred has the cat. The solution is found by elimination. From (1), neither Eliza nor Ben have the parrot. Using (2), Fred does not have a parrot, owl or parakeet. From (3), Debbie does not have the parakeet. Condition (4) gives the information that Ben had neither the cat nor the dog. From (5), Eliza had neither the owl, cat nor parakeet. Using (6), The owl and parakeet can be eliminated from both Anita and Ben. This means that the parakeet can only be Chuck, so he can be eliminated from parrot, fish, owl, dog, and cat. This gives Debbie as the owl, so she can be eliminated from parrot, fish, dog and cat. Anita must be the parrot and Ben the fish so that subsequent eliminations lead to Fred with the cat and Eliza with the dog.

Alien Ages

	Name	Race	Planet	Age
1	Hoot	Crisp	Grunt	706
2	Eek	Fodder	Flip	385
3	Doodah	Bunter	Esther	32
4	Ting	Winky	Dorb	213
5	Peep	Tartan	Booper	503
6	Bleep	Polyp	Parp	897

From (6), Esther can be at 1, 2 or 3. If at 1 (with 213 at 2 and Polyp at 4), from (3), Doodah can only be at 4 (with 385 at 3 and Tartan at 6), but now there's nowhere to fit (4). If Esther is at 2 (with 213 at 3 and Polyp at 5), from (2), Booper can be at 4 or 6. If Booper is at 6 (with 32 at 4 and Eek at 3), Grunt must be at 5, as it is the only thing than can still be correct in the Planet column, and then there's nowhere to fit (5). If Booper is at 4, from (4), 706 must be at 1, and there's nowhere to fit (3). So Esther is at 3 (with 213 at 3 and Polyp at 6). From (2), Booper would fit at 4 or 5, but at 4 both Esther and Booper would be correct, so Booper is at 5 (with Eek at 2 and 32 at 3). From (3), Doodah must be at 3 (with 385 at 2 and

Tartan at 5). From (4), Ting must be at 4 (with 706 at 1). From (5), Bunter must be at 3 (with Peep at 5 and Parp at 6). From (1), Grunt is at 1 and Fodder at 2. In the first column, Peep is correct at 5, Bleep is wrong at 1 so must be at 6 with Hoot at 1. For the second column, Bunter is correct at 3, Crisp is wrong at 4 so must be at 1 leaving Winky at 4. Esther is correct in the third column; Dorb is incorrect at 2 so must be at 4 leaving Flip at 2. For the fourth column, 385 is correct, 897 is wrong at 5 so must be at 6 with 503 at 5.

Animal Races

	Animal	Name	Prize
1	frog	Lorna	carrot
2	badger	Harry	Porsche
3	antelope	Ian	radiator
4	dog	George	microwave
5	elephant	Jenny	television
6	cat	Karen	spoon

From (4), Ian can be at 1, 2 or 3. If he is at 1, from (5), Lorna can be at 2 or 4. At 2, condition (3) is violated, and at 4, from (2), Harry cannot fit. If Ian is at 2, from (5), Lorna can only be at 3 but then condition (3) is again violated. So Ian is at 3 (with dog at 4 and spoon at 6). From (5), Lorna can be at 1 or 4. At 4, condition (3) is violated. So Lorna is at 1 (with antelope at 3 and Porsche at 2). From (2), Harry can only be at 2 (with elephant at 5 and microwave at 4). In the first column, antelope is correct, badger is wrong at 1, cannot be at 6 due to (1), so must be at 2. Frog is wrong at 6 so can only be at 1, leaving cat at 6. For the second column, Harry is correct at 2, George is wrong at 5, cannot be at 6 due to (1) so must be at 4. Jenny is wrong at 6 so must be at 5 with Karen at 6. In the third column, microwave is correct at 4. From (3), since Ian is not carrot then carrot is not third. Carrot is wrong at 5, so must be at 1. This means that television, which is wrong at 3, must be at 5 with radiator at 3.

Best Book Prize

	Verb 1	Noun	Verb 2	Adverb
1	Shooting	Puddings	Jumping	Cruelly
2	Making	Cakes	Hopping	Stupidly
3	Killing	Flies	Running	Loudly
4	Hitting	Sharks	Laughing	Quickly

From (6), Cakes can be at 1, 2 or 3. If it is at 1 (with Running at 2), from (5), Jumping can be at 1 or 3. Both cases violate condition (1). If Cakes is at 3 (with Running at 4), from (2), Sharks can be at 2 or 4. At 2, both Sharks and Cakes are correct (invalid), and at 4, Sharks is placed with Running, violating condition (4). So Cakes is not at 3 and must be at 2 (with Running at 3). From (5), Jumping can be at 1 or 2, but 2 is ruled out since this violates (1). So Jumping must be at 1 (with Making at 2). From (2), Sharks can be at 3 or 4. At 3, Sharks and Running are together violating (4). This leaves Sharks at 4 (with Loudly at 3). From (3), Killing can fit at 1 or 3. At 1, both Killing and Making are correct (invalid). So Killing is at 3 (with Quickly at 4). In the first column, Making is correct at 2, Shooting is wrong at 4 so must be at 1 leaving Hitting at 4. For the second column, only Puddings can be correct at 1, so Flies is at 3. Running is correct at 3 in the third column, Hopping is wrong at 4 so must be at 2 leaving Laughing at 4. Finally, Quickly is right at 4, Stupidly is wrong at 1, so must be at 2 with Cruelly at 1.

Court Napping

	Title	Name	Favorite Game
1	King	Driftoff	rummy
2	Princess	Mutter	hearts
3	Earl	Bleereye	gin
4	Queen	Outovit	poker
5	Duke	Yawny	bridge

From (4), King can be at 1, 2 or 3. If he is at 2, from (2), Outovit can be at 1 or 3. If it is 1 (with bridge at 2), the coincidence of King and bridge violates (3). If it is 3, from (1), Mutter can only be at 2 and the coincidence of King and

Mutter also violates (3). So King is not at 2. If King is at 3, from (2), Outavit can be at 1, 2 or 4. If it is 1, from (1), Mutter can be at 3 or 4. At 3, condition (3) is violated, and at 4 (with Earl at 5), both King and Earl are correct (invalid). If Outavit is at 2 (with bridge at 3), then condition (3) is violated. If Outavit is at 4, from (5), Princess can only fit at 1, so that both King and Princess are correct (invalid). So King is not at 3 and must be at 1 (with hearts at 2 and Bleery at 3). From (2), Outavit can be at 2 or 4. If it is 2, from (1), Mutter can be at 1 or 4. If Mutter is at 1 then (3) is violated. If it is 4 then both Bleery and Mutter are correct in the second column (invalid). So Outavit is not at 2 and must be at 4 (with bridge at 5). From (5), Princess must be at 2 (with poker at 4). From (1), Earl can only be at 3 (with Mutter at 2). In the first column, only Queen at 4 can be correct so Duke is at 5. For the Name column, Bleery is correct at 3, Yawny is wrong at 1 so must be at 5, leaving Driftoff at 1. In the third column, only gin at 3 can be correct, leaving rummy at 1.

The Witch's Pudding

The order was sheep droppings, crushed pig's ear, dirty snow, castor oil, and dishwater. Let dishwater be A, castor oil B, dirty snow C, crushed pig's ear D, and sheep droppings E. The only pairs that are less than 50% of the cauldron volume are CD, DE, CE (order unimportant). The only possibilities having C two places after E and A later than B which is later than D are EDCBA, DEBCA, DBEAC. Only the first of these has the second and third places occupied by one of the above pairs.

The Colored Ties

Alan has green, Bert has yellow, and Callum has yellow. If a person claims he has one of two colors, either he sees one of the other two as red (leaving yellow or green for himself) or he sees two yellow (leaving red or green for himself). For a person to say he must be one of three colors he must see yellow and green or two green. When two people make this claim, no red can be present. Hence Alan has seen no red and must have seen two yellow and his own color must be green.

The Four Badges

Alice has yellow, Barney has yellow, Carrie has green and Denzil has red. From Alice's statement, Barney and Carrie can respectively have YY, GG, YG or GY but Carrie's statement reduces these possibilities to YY or YG, so Barney must have yellow. From Barney's statement, Alice, Carrie and Denzil share RYG but from Carrie's statement, neither Alice nor Denzil can have green, so the green must belong to Carrie. The red and yellow are then shared between Alice and Denzil. From Denzil's statement, two of Alice, Barney and Carrie have identical colors (to leave just two colors for Denzil) so this means that Alice has yellow and Denzil has red.

The Four Robbers

A   B   C   D

From (3), hair B can be at 2 or 3. If it is at 2 (with nose B at 1 and mouth D at 3) then, from (2), mouth A can only be at 2. This means that no item can be correct in the mouth row. If hair B is at 3 (with nose B at 2 and mouth D at 4) then from (1), hair C can be at 2 or 4. At 2, there can be either none or two correct in the hair row (invalid). So hair C is at 4 (with eyes C at 3). From (2), nose C can be at either 3 or 4. At 3, both nose B and nose C are correct in the noses row (invalid). So nose C is at 4 (with eyes D at 2 and mouth A at 3). In the hair row, only hair A can be correct (at 1), so hair D is at 2. For the eyes, eyes C are correct at 3, eyes A are wrong at 1 so are at 4, with eyes B at 1. For the noses, nose B is correct at 2, nose A is wrong at 1 so is at 3, leaving nose D at 1. In the mouth row, mouth D is correct at 4, mouth B is wrong at 2 so is at 1, with mouth C at 2.

The Beauty Contest

	Contestant	House Name	Occupation
1	Ms. Slapinum	Wyewurry	sheep shearer
2	Mrs. Wowie	Duncheatin	bullfighter
3	Ms. Myafare	Outasugar	mud wrestler

From (3), Ms. Myafare cannot be at 1, so from (2), Ms. Slapinum is at 1. The first column cannot now have all three correct and neither can the third column, since from (3), bullfighter cannot occupy 3. So the second column has all three correct. From (1), since Ms. Slapinum is at 1, Ms. Myafare is at Outasugar which is at 3. From (3), bullfighter is at 2. So Mrs. Wowie is at 2 and the first column has none correct. This leaves the third column with one correct. This must be sheep shearer at 1, leaving mud wrestler at 3.

INDEX

What Is Mensa?

Mensa
The High IQ Society

Mensa is the international society for people with a high IQ. We have more than 100,000 members in over 40 countries worldwide.

Anyone with an IQ score in the top two percent of population is eligible to become a member of Mensa—are you the "one in 50" we've been looking for?

Mensa membership offers an excellent range of benefits:

- Networking and social activities nationally and around the world;
- Special Interest Groups (hundreds of chances to pursue your hobbies and interests—from art to zoology!);
- Monthly International Journal, national magazines, and regional newsletters;
- Local meetings—from game challenges to food and drink;
- National and international weekend gatherings and conferences;
- Intellectually stimulating lectures and seminars;
- Access to the worldwide SIGHT network for travelers and hosts.

For more information about American Mensa:
www.us.mensa.org
Telephone: (800) 66-MENSA
American Mensa Ltd.
1229 Corporate Drive West
Arlington, TX 76006-6103
USA

For more information about British Mensa (UK and Ireland):
www.mensa.org.uk
Telephone: +44 (0) 1902 772771
E-mail: enquiries@mensa.org.uk
British Mensa Ltd.
St. John's House, St. John's Square
Wolverhampton WV2 4AH
United Kingdom

For more information about Mensa International:
www.mensa.org
Mensa International
15 The Ivories
6-8 Northampton Street
Islington, London N1 2HY, United Kingdom